Sketches of the Life and Ministry of the Rev. C. H. Spurgeon

by

George John Stevenson

Sketches of the Life and Ministry of the Rev. C. H. Spurgeon
Including Anecdotes and Incidents of Travel; Biographical Notices of Former Pastors; Historical Sketch of Park-street Chapel; and an Outline of Mr. Spurgeon's Articles of Faith.

First published in 1857

Current edition published in 2013 by
Victory Baptist Press
Milton, FL - USA

ISBN 978-1-940791-91-3

This book has been edited and revised for design purposes as well as text readability.

CONTENTS

INTRODUCTION

Popular favor has seldom been shown to any man so extensively, and so spontaneously, as it has been to the Rev. Charles Haddon Spurgeon. Although some of the worst feelings of human nature have long been in active exercise to check the benevolent labors of this philanthropic, youthful divine, an overseeing and an overruling providence has directed the issue. The favors of friends and the frowns of foes have together resulted in promoting the great work for which this modern Whitefield seems especially raised up, namely, to preach the gospel in a manner, which shall secure its welcome to the hearts of multitudes who have hitherto disregarded it.

Many have been the inquiries, which have been made respecting Mr. Spurgeon's antecedents. One asks to which of the universities he belongs; another wonders how so young a man obtained holy orders; a third puts the question plainly, "Who ordained the young man?" A page would not suffice to enumerate the interrogatives we have ourselves heard from all classes of people; from the plain-spoken Englishman, from the penetrating Scotchman, from the mirthful son of Erin and from not a few of our transatlantic brethren. Indeed, we have had this kind of verbal investigation continued, with the greatest possible relish by the inquirer, for an hour together, without any apparent abatement in interest. In some instances, the desire for information has led to a succession of queries so varied and so strange, that a prudent man would rather remain silent than try to satisfy such prurient curiosity. In this great London, thousands of voices have repeated the question in one day—"Who is this Spurgeon?" And, to many, a negative was not an answer; so that where positive information of a reliable kind could not be obtained, imagination has too often supplied its place, to the injury of both the subject of this sketch, and the work in which he is engaged. So intense was the desire for information respecting Mr. Spurgeon during several months, that whoever would risk a few pages of biographical anecdotes, historical incidents or doctrinal peculiarities, at the price of a penny, was sure to sell the work by the thousands. These transient phantoms have now all passed away, having satisfied the mere inquisitor, while the seekers after knowledge are still eagerly desiring to know more. The number of these is still a multitude. Were it otherwise, we should not see, each successive Sunday morning, from ten to twelve thousand persons, some from every part of London and its expansive suburbs, including many from the provinces, gathered to worship in the great Surrey Music Hall. Nor is this spirit of inquiry unnatural or wonderful. The wonder would be far greater were it otherwise. In the Church of England, such instances of youthful divines and youthful oratory are unknown. In the established church, the best read student, the most fluent orator, the soundest divine, or the most earnest Christian in our universities must pass his twenty-third year before he is allowed to exercise his gifts in publicly calling sinners to repentance. Our Southwark divine, on the contrary, before twenty-three summers have swept over his head, has not only been allowed to preach publicly, and with authority, but with a power and a success, which, considering the shortness of the period, really has no parallel. Long before an English churchman is considered of sufficient age and discretion to be presented to the bishop for ordination, our modern Whitefield has been a successful preacher for several years; so successful, indeed, that there are numerous towns and villages in the land in which his well known voice has pealed out its "come and welcome" to congregations numbering not hundreds only, but repeatedly ten thousand persons, and from among whom some hundreds have been gathered out of the world and infolded in the church of Christ.

We have met and conversed with English clergymen who are well aware of the secret of the success of this eminent preacher, and who righteously covet, to some extent, his gifts and his honors. There is a charm about the young man, which wins the good will at the least of by far the greater majority of those who hear him. The existence of this charm is patent to the world, and its influence is already felt in every country where the Saxon character and the English language exist. There is one country where the good done by this laborious minister would not be recognized—but it is because Italian, not Saxon, blood flows in the veins of the inhabitants.

Mr. Spurgeon's popularity is both wonderful and natural. There exists but few instances, in either ancient or modern times, of men, so young, producing an influence for good to his fellow men on so large a scale, as in the instance before us. One of the youngest persons ever sent out into the work of the ministry among the Methodists was the late learned Dr. Adam Clarke. While yet a "youth in his teens," we find him appointed to a circuit so wide, that he had to preach in a different place, once at the least, during every day in each successive month. Although tall in person, yet so slender, he was generally denominated "the little boy" preacher. There are many points of resemblance in the early preaching career of this eminent scholar, divine, and Christian, to those connected with Mr. Spurgeon. The almost tender years of both preachers prompted many to go and hear for themselves. In both cases, large multitudes of young persons of both sexes gathered together and formed a large proportion of the preacher's audience. In both cases, many persons of age and experience stood aloof for a time, throwing out innuendoes, cautions, and warnings, and in both cases such men lived long enough to acknowledge their error.

Another preacher among the Wesleyans presents to us, in some respects, a parallel case to Mr. Spurgeon's. Of the Rev. Richard Watson, we read, that "impelled by a conviction of duty, and an intense zeal for the spiritual good of mankind, the day after he was fifteen years of age, Richard Watson preached his first sermon in a cottage a few miles from Lincoln." He continued to preach, prompted by the same excellent motives, with great success, for nearly forty years. There is, however, one point in the cases of these preachers that deserves notice more particularly. In many points, the career of the two young Methodist preachers, and the young Baptist minister, very nearly agree—in age, learning, zeal, piety, and success, they are all three remarkable, and are very near parallels. In the opposition to which they were all subject, and the persecution, which was carried on against them with a very high hand, they are not dissimilar, excepting in this particular. The persecutors of the last century were the ordained clergy; Mr. Spurgeon's persecutors are not the clergy, though report represents some of them as jealous, others as envious—but persecution has come only from the press, or from that portion of it, which would like to make religion a lifeless formality, and which shrinks alike from both conscience and eternity. The clergy of our day not only do not persecute the Southwark evangelist, they rather seek and embrace every occasion which offers to go and hear for themselves, and where they cannot go and hear, we know that very many of them read Mr. Spurgeon's published discourses with great satisfaction and pleasure. Here then, we think we have an instance of true greatness, a young divine, whose powerful voice, whose untiring zeal, whose ardent love of his work, prompt him to "labors more abundant" in trying to do good alike to the bodies and the souls of the greatest number of his fellow-creatures.

In the late Rev. William Jay, we have another instance of a very young man giving himself to the service of the ministry. In an old, almost forgotten book, called *The Triumph of Faith*, we find a reference to the employment of young Jay, at about the age of sixteen, in publicly proclaiming the truths of the gospel to perishing sinners. His career of usefulness, on a large scale, continued for more than half a century. Nor is our good friend of New Park-street alone in our own times, as a very young man, raised up by Almighty God to rouse the slumbering churches of England. Pastors of churches! ye who have had flocks without increase for many years past, God calls you, by the example of these young men, to try the power of faith living, acting faith. Try it! God has owned and prospered the zealous labors of these young men, and he will continue to own them. Imitate their example. Let your motto be—onwards! Faith is a very powerful agency; use it, test it, exhaust it, if you can; faith removes mountains, and "laughs at impossibilities."

Great revivals of religion have generally emanated from the zeal, painstaking and self-denial of young persons. The two Wesleys were young when, 160 years ago, they commenced their great work. Whitefield was young when his extraordinary labors and eloquence were the means of gathering multitudes out of the world and enfolding them in the church of Christ. Jay, Clarke, Finney, and many others might be named in proof of this point, and such results should be looked for more than they have been, as evidence of dutiful obedience to that God who, having forgiven much, deserves diligent and earnest service in return.

NEW PARK-STREET CHAPEL

This edifice, now so well known by multitudes in every part of England, is quite of modern construction, not having existed a quarter of a century, while the church formed within its walls is venerable alike for both age and influence. From the early annals of nonconformity, we learn, that as early as the year 1652, a division took place in one of the oldest Baptist churches in London, owing to some practices in which the members could not agree. In those troublesome times, large bodies of dissenters could not meet together without peril; nor could small bodies make much ado about their disagreements, fearing the strong arm of an unjust power, exercised very unscrupulously at that period, against all who did not belong to the church of the state. We shall not here trace the outline of the disputes referred to; it may suffice to say that, according to Crosby, certain practices, considered to be disorderly, caused the division referred to, and several members united themselves together, holding their meetings from time to time at each other's houses, by private arrangement, in the parish of Horsleydown, Southwark.

The chief brother, or elder, connected with the seceders, was a Mr. William Rider. Under his pastoral care and advice, they were formed into a small church, and for a period of five years maintained "the unity of the Spirit in the bonds of peace." Though few in numbers, they were of considerable influence, some of the members being among the merchants of that age, and what was of greater importance, the congregation had a character for sound judgment, united with solid and earnest piety. Such influences, in those times, in their judicious exercise, never failed to accomplish much lasting good. In the selection of their pastor depended mainly their success, though their existence as a church never seems to have been in peril.

In the year 1668, a change took place in the pastorate of this small church. A self-taught man, a native of Buckinghamshire, then not thirty years old, although experienced as a pastor, was called to preside over the little Zion. Benjamin Keach, who was baptized by immersion in his fifteenth year, and who, at the age of eighteen, was called to the ministry, after enduring losses, bereavements, punishment in the pillory, and who, in the midst and through all his severe trials, was faithful alike to his great Master and to his principles, was called from the country to preside over this flourishing church in 1668. For a period of thirty-six years, this exemplary divine ministered to their spiritual wants, and during several years, he was much occupied in writing and publishing works in defense of the principles he believed and preached—works that remain, to this day, an honor both to the head and to the heart of that good man. His whole life seems to have been one of earnestness, and his aim, to set forth the vital power of personal religion. As a Christian, as a divine, as an author and as a controversialist, Benjamin Keach must rank among the giants of those days. He died July 18, 1704, aged sixty-three, and his body was laid in the burial ground belonging to the Baptists, in the park, Southwark. In the early part of his ministry, the church had met for worship in a private house on Tooley Street, and in that dwelling-house was this man of God solemnly ordained by prayer and the laying-on of hands. A few years later, we find the king, Charles II, granting privileges to Protestant dissenters, one of which enabled the congregation to erect a meeting-house upon the Horsleydown, on the east side of old London Bridge. The blessing of God was so abundantly shown, in answer to simple faith and earnest prayer, that the new preaching place soon became too small, and a larger edifice was set up, in which accommodation was provided for nearly a thousand persons. Here, however, division entered, and some of the members left Mr. Keach and joined themselves into a body, forming a church that established itself, and still exists, at Maze Pond, close to the terminus of the Brighton railway.

Mr. Benjamin Stinton was then chosen pastor of the church. In sorrow had this church originated, and through sorrowful times, had it struggled and survived. The name of Benjamin belonging to its two early pastors is indicative of the character of the times, and the origin of its existence. Benoni, the son of sorrow, was altered by the patriarch Jacob to Benjamin, the son of my right hand; and truly did these two Benjamins show themselves to be workers or helpers together with God as dutiful and diligent sons, in the great work of preaching the gospel. Mr. B. Stinton died in the year 1719.

His successor was the eminent and learned John Gill, D.D., F.A.S. This excellent scholar and divine was born November 19, 1697, at Kettering, and had been the pastor of a Baptist church in that place. He removed to Higham Ferrers in the year 1717, and thence to the church assembling at Goat Street, Horsleydown, where he was ordained its pastor, March 22, 1719. A difference at once arose on the selection of Dr. Gill, the majority of the members being against the doctor, and another separation was the consequence. When the lease of the old chapel had expired, the majority formed themselves into another church, and erected for themselves another meeting-house in Unicorn Yard, while those forming Dr. Gill's section assembled in the old chapel until the year 1757.

It then became necessary to enlarge their borders. Another new chapel, or meeting-house, as they were then designated, was erected for the doctor's congregation in Carter Lane, Tooley Street, near to London Bridge. The learning and piety of this eminent divine soon attracted a large congregation, and the reward of a sanctified intellect was a numerous and influential church, standing prominently out as one of the chief Baptist congregations in the land. Dr. Gill was the author of several important works. His great work was an exposition of the Bible, in nine folio volumes; his other works are still considered worthy of a prominent place in the library of the theologian and the scholar. The blessing of Divine Providence rested eminently on this flourishing cause, and the pastor lived to celebrate his jubilee as minister of that church and people. For the long period of fifty-two years, the gospel-trumpet sounded among that favored people by this venerable man; and never were the doctrines of free grace more successfully and plainly preached than during the protracted ministry of this eminent servant of God. After a lengthened illness, Dr. Gill died on October 14, 1771.

Another separation took place at this period, many of the members withdrawing and forming a church in Dean Street, which afterward established itself in Trinity Street, where it still flourishes.

A young man of only twenty years, from the Baptist Academy at Bristol, was invited to preach in the now destitute church of Carter Lane for seven Sundays. John Rippon, the youth we have named, was born near Tiverton, in Devonshire, April 29, 1751. After preaching for one year on trial, he was ordained pastor of the church in November 1773. Here, he continued to labor with unabated zeal and fidelity during the long period of sixty-three years. Dr. Gill was their pastor for nearly 54 years, which, added to the pastorate of Dr. Rippon, gives a period of 117 years, during which this church had only two pastors. In the year 1787, Dr. Rippon published a selection of 1,174 hymns, which has had an extensive circulation. This selection is still used by the descendants of the doctor's congregation in New Park-street chapel. In the year 1790, the doctor commenced publishing a *Baptist Register*, giving accounts of all the Baptist churches and ministers in the land. This useful work was continued for twelve years, and then was suffered to die. Contemporary with such men as Toplady, Romaine, Berridge, the Wesleys, John Fletcher, Rowland Hill, and others of great energy, strong faith, and sincere piety, yet Dr. Rippon maintained a distinguished position among these talented divines, and he was considered one of the most popular preachers among the modern Calvinists of his day; and his church was the largest belonging to the Baptists in London. It numbered 400 members at the commencement of this century. His memory is cherished with much affection by many still living in Southwark; and even men of the world we have heard speak of him as the good man of the neighborhood. So great was his love and zeal for the bodies, as well as the souls of his congregation, that he commenced a subscription for the erection of alms-houses, and he succeeded in his work. First, a house was taken near the chapel, after which three alms-houses were erected and called after the founder. A benevolent lady who was a member of Dr. Rippon's church, left money to endow and keep the alms-houses in repair. The property is vested in trustees. They were removed from Carter Lane when New London Bridge was built, and others erected in New Park-street, adjoining the new chapel, in 1832. Other interesting particulars respecting these alms-houses we have been favored with, through the kindness of Miss Fanny Gray, one of the inmates, and deaconess of the chapel, we are obliged to omit. On a tablet placed on the first of these dwellings, is the following inscription:—

DR. RIPPON'S ALMS-HOUSES,
Formerly in Carter Lane, Tooley-street, having been taken down for the approaches to New London Bridge, these were erected in their stead.
Anno Domini MDCCCXXXII

He died a few days before Christmas in the year 1836, aged eighty-five years, and was buried in Bunhill Fields, which event was solemnly improved by the late Dr. Cox, of Hackney, delivering a funeral oration in New Park-street chapel.

This now celebrated chapel was erected out of the purchase-money given by the city of London for the Carter Lane chapel, and was opened May 6, 1833, only three years before the venerable divine was summoned to mansions above. Mrs. Morgan, his much respected housekeeper, still survives as one of the occupants of Dr. Rippon's alms-houses, which are represented in the engraving. The chapel has been enlarged during the ministry of its present pastor, to which further reference will be hereafter made.

The Rev. C. Room, who had long assisted Dr. Rippon, occupied the pulpit for some time. He was followed by Dr. Angus, who was ordained pastor, but who left Park-street after two years to enter on a wider sphere of labor, and who is now filling an important duty in the Baptist College for training young ministers. The Rev. James Smith next became the pastor of the New Park-street church. During his nine years' ministry, the church prospered much and increased greatly. On his removal to Cheltenham, where, as an author and an instructive popular preacher, he has earned for himself a good reputation, the Rev. W. Walters, now of Halifax, accepted a call to the church. These frequent changes had not a good effect. The number of church-members, although increased by Mr. Smith's ministry, was comparatively small. From the extreme of prosperity, and from the highest point of eminence and influence, the church at New Park-street had greatly diminished in numbers, until the congregation did not occupy more than half the seats in the new chapel, and the income had become insufficient to sustain the pastor, and pay the ordinary expenses of the place. No part of England was less able to endure such a reverse as had come upon this once flourishing cause, than the locality around this place of worship. Celebrated as the immediate neighborhood had been for centuries for the Globe Theatre of Shakespeare, the bear-garden of Elizabeth, and though last, but not least, the place where John Bunyan had often preached, the decline of the cause of God was not only to be regretted, but also deplored. It was the source of many anxious and earnest prayers; and Divine Providence was preparing and training just the man every way adapted to meet the wants of that extremely poor neighborhood. Mr. Walters was pastor about two years.

A Sunday school anniversary meeting was held in Zion chapel, Cambridge. A very young man was called upon to speak at that meeting. Another young man was present, himself a stranger, heard that speech, and was deeply impressed by it. Shortly afterward, the young man in the audience, and one of the deacons of New Park-street chapel, meet each other. One recites a tale of lamentation; the other delivers a message of hope. Time passes; it is summer 1853; but

> "God's providences ripen fast,
> Unfolding every hour."

The young speaker at Cambridge is recommended to the New Park-street deacon; hope succeeds; faith is strengthened; the young speaker is applied to, and soon after, while yet in his "teens," becomes the appointed pastor of the once largest Baptist church in London. This young man is the REV. CHARLES HADDON SPURGEON.

WHO IS THIS SPURGEON?

To this inquiry, many have in vain sought for an answer. The following pages will furnish what we think will be received as demonstrative evidence that Mr. Spurgeon has been raised up, and specially trained, by Divine Providence, to accomplish a great moral and spiritual work, by promoting the well-being of both the bodies and the souls of the multitudes who almost daily throng to hear him.

The villages of England, more than the cities, have the honor of producing our great men. The city may be favorable to early development, and sometimes to precocity in talent; but it too often wanes ere it has reached maturity. In the village, the faculties develop themselves as nature forms them; in the city, a thousand delusive influences are constantly working on the minds of the young; and for one who adopts a course, which is at once upright and successful, a thousand go wrong. The whole population of Kelvedon, in Essex, in which Mr. Spurgeon was born, does not number 2,000 souls, while his Sabbath-morning congregations often number 10,000 persons; so that almost weekly he preaches to five times more persons than were contained in the place which gave him birth. Kelvedon has had advantages in religion, which have influenced the population. For more than fifty years, the same clergyman preached in the parish church, and his life has been in accordance with his preaching. The Rev. Charles Dalton lately celebrated his jubilee as the incumbent of that village, and his long life of consistent piety has not been without its all-pervading influence on the villagers. Mr. Spurgeon is of nonconformist descent, and entered this world on June 19, 1834. His venerable grandfather, the Rev. James Spurgeon, still lives, and continues his ministerial duties as pastor of an Independent church at Stambourne, near Halstead, in Essex. The father of our Southwark divine is Mr. John Spurgeon, second son of the forenamed Rev. James Spurgeon, now of Colchester, who, although occupied as a layman during the week, is the pastor of a small Independent church at Tollesbury, in Essex. The mother of Mr. Spurgeon was the youngest sister of Charles Parker Jarvis, Esq., of Colchester, a woman remarkable for piety, usefulness and humility.

Here, then, we have presumptive, and we can safely add positive, evidence of the example of both personal and family religion, for at least two generations, operating in the formation of the mind of our youthful divine Praying parents! Oh! the charm, the power of such influences! Parents, ye who fear God, "let your light so shine" before your children, that they may follow after godliness in imitating you. The father of George Whitefield was the son of a clergyman, but George was born at a well-known inn, kept by Thomas Whitefield, in Gloucester. It is somewhat remarkable, that while George Whitefield is known as the pot-boy of his father's inn, the birth-place of Mr. Spurgeon (called the modern Whitefield), in Kelvedon, has, since the removal of Mr. John Spurgeon to Colchester, been used as a wayside inn also. Here are both extremes and parallels. In both cases, religion is a family possession, and the power of prayer is expansive. Careful home training, pervaded by the influence of personal and family religion, is capable of, and has resulted in, an immeasurable amount of good.

At a very early period, the infant Spurgeon, who was the first grandchild in the family, was removed from his father's residence at Kelvedon, to his grandfather's at Stambourne, and placed under the care of Ann Spurgeon, his father's sister. It is needless to add with what delight the venerable pair welcomed the stranger in the family. Miss Ann Spurgeon was at that time not in a good state of health, and both the grandparents of the infant believed that the care of the child would have a beneficial effect on the health of their daughter. The result proved the wisdom of their decision. Under the fostering care of the aunt, and the solicitude of the grandparents, the health of the former gradually improving, the child grew in strength, and soon became the admired and beloved of all who knew him; Affection, blended with personal piety, was the watchword of the household; Aunt Ann loved and cherished most tenderly her infant charge, and she received, as her reward, the sincere affection of her adopted child. The affection between the two became as strong as between a child and its parent, and "Mother Ann," and "Stepson Charles," are terms as familiar and endearing in this case as are the terms mother and child in ordinary cases. The first dawnings of reason were observed, and care was taken to inform and instruct by such degrees as the opening faculties could receive. From infancy, the mind of the child seems to have been formed after nature's model. When but an infant, he would divert himself for hours together with a book of pictures, although unable to either speak plain or read. His love of books dates from the first openings of his mind. One of the books that served to amuse the many hours of early childhood, contained, among other illustrations, a portrait of Bonner, Bishop of London. He was informed that Bishop Bonner was a persecutor of some of the servants of God; and although so young, an effect was produced on his mind, which will never be erased, and the child manifested such a dislike to the name, that he always called that picture, as a term of derision and in righteous indignation, "Old Bonner." This is powerful censure from a boy so young. To this period of his life may be traced the origin of that intense abhorrence of tyranny in every form and under every name, to which Mr. Spurgeon sometimes gives utterance.

Another feature characteristic of Mr. Spurgeon is traceable to this early period. Even in infancy, he manifested a marked attachment to those who were said, or even supposed, to be the children of God. He had a special preference to the house of God. To him it was not merely a pleasure to go, and a source of joy to remain, but it was a positive delight. When he had acquired the art of reading, his joy in being able to unite in the worship of God in the sanctuary scarcely knew any bounds. This feeling does not abate, for we find, by the public papers, that he is preaching in some part of England almost every day, and in some cases in two different towns in one day. Unlike most children, play had not the charm for the youthful Spurgeon, which a book had; and when he had learned to gather the sense of a book, his desire for the acquirement of knowledge amounted to a passion, so that considerable restraint had to be exercised to prevent injury to the mind of the young scholar. In this respect, there is a remarkable parallel between Mr. Spurgeon and the late Duke of Wellington. Of the latter we are informed, that while his school-fellows enjoyed their games, he often stood aloof, his mind apparently occupied with something less volatile than play. As the child, so, generally, will the man be. Before the child was six years old, he could read well, with a tone and emphasis beyond his age. Give him his book, and his liberty, and when he was wanted, he was always found in seclusion with his book, enjoying that which was, to most children, only drudgery. Here it was that he laid the foundation of that varied and extended acquaintance with the writings of good old John Bunyan, B. Baxter, and others of that period. There is a charm about the works of the tinker of Bedford, which has captivated millions of people, young and old. Dr. Johnson has written that there are three books, which every man can take up with the same relish for the second as for the first reading: these are the Bible, *Pilgrim's Progress* and *Robinson Crusoe*. No wonder then that our young friend was captivated with these works, and read them with eager delight.

Christian fellowship is one of the great privileges of all the children of God. During the early years of Mr. Spurgeon's life, spent in the family of his grandfather, there were many occasions when various members of the church met at the residence of their pastor, and there taking sweet counsel together, enjoyed the "communion of saints." On many of these Sabbath meetings, which are remembered with delight by the friends at Stambourne, the grandchild of the pastor astonished many by his questions and conversation. Often he would propose a subject, and offer remarks upon it, which astonished much older and experienced persons.

From infancy, he was remarkable for decision of character. And his decision was taken for God. There was no halting between two opinions. He boldly and steadfastly maintained his choice. When under six years of age, he saw in the village a man who professed religion mixed up with a number of others known to be ungodly men. He felt a desire to reprove the professor, and in the name and in the strength of the God he served, he boldly went up to the man and addressed him in these words: "Elijah, what doest thou here?" The man was dumb under the reproof; and the boy came away with a conviction that he had done his duty. God always rewards those who serve him faithfully. Self-possession is a feature strongly marked in Mr. Spurgeon. His cool and collected behavior during the unfortunate Surrey Gardens catastrophe was the astonishment of many. Shortly before that event, while preaching to a large audience in Islington, he made a sudden pause in the service, and remarked, with great firmness of manner, "There are two persons near the door, if they do not behave better, I must desire the police to remove them," and went on with the service as though there had been no interruption. And, again, with an audience of some 10,000 persons before him, only a few weeks ago, in the Surrey Hall, after expounding the first of two lessons, he announced the chapter of the second lesson, and then said, "If I make a short pause between the lessons, it will give an opportunity for those persons who have their hats on, to take them off in the house of God." He preached that morning from the text, "Wist ye not that I must be about my Father's business?" And one more suitable to describe the persevering and untiring labors of this devoted servant of God could not well have been chosen.

Young men! Young ministers! let the same mind be in you! Decision for God and boldness in His service, will bring to you a present reward, great or small in proportion to your zeal.

During the seven years passed so happily at Stambourne, the education of their grandson was not a subject of great concern to the grandparents of our youthful divine. His mental development was already considerably in advance of his years, and his moral faculties were of a character to cause but little concern for the future. For most of this information respecting the early years of Mr. Spurgeon we are indebted to his grandfather. But there are two sentences in the account furnished by the Rev. James Spurgeon, relating to his grandson, which deserve to be written in letters of gold. Of the great and good George Washington we read, that when charged by his father with doing a mischievous, though only a boyish, action in his garden, the noble boy said, "It was me, father, I dare not tell a lie." Of Charles H. Spurgeon, his grandfather writes: "I do not remember ever hearing of his speaking anything but the truth." And again: "I cannot remember that we had ever an occasion to correct him for any false tale." Here, then, is a model for children to imitate. Always speak the truth: fear a lie. Nothing makes a man a greater coward than falsehood; and tale-bearers are always nervous and in fear. Mr. Spurgeon is fearless of man in his denunciations of sin. This righteous boldness is traceable to a source, which is a tower of strength to any minister—he is a man of TRUTH.

When he was about seven years old, Mr. Spurgeon returned to his father's home. During his residence at Stambourne, his parents had removed from Kelvedon to Colchester, in which town Mr. John Spurgeon was occupied. He was at once placed in a respectable school, conducted by Mr. Henry Lewis. The head usher in the school was Mr. Leeding, who afterward removed from Colchester to Cambridge, and there opened a school for young gentlemen. Four years were spent in the school at Colchester, and here the ready mind of the pupil soon attracted the special attention of Mr. Leeding. To this gentleman, our young friend is indebted for nearly all the knowledge he acquired which could be there communicated. In every branch of knowledge to which he devoted his attention, C.H. Spurgeon was sure to become master of it; and invariably at the examinations, our young friend was the successful prize-man.

When he was about ten years of age, he was spending a vacation with his grandsire at Stambourne. The anniversary sermons for the Missionary Society were preached in his grandfather's chapel while he was there. The preacher was the late Rev. Richard Knill. This earnest and devoted servant of God has left behind him a memory for good, which will be cherished with much affection for many years. Inscribed on the portrait of this self-denying missionary is the motto, which indicated the intensity of his love for his work: "Brethren! the heathen are perishing; shall we let them perish?

God forbid. Richard Knill." Knowing this of the preacher, it is not wonderful that he discerned in the grandson of the venerable Spurgeon the germs of his future distinction. Mr. Knill remained with the village pastor on the night of the anniversary.

The following particulars we give from a communication kindly supplied by the Rev. James Spurgeon, of Stambourne.

> "Before family prayer, my grandson read a chapter out of the Scriptures, and our friend Knill was very much pleased, and said, 'I have heard old ministers and young ones read well, but never did I hear a little boy read so correctly before.' He called him to his side, laid his venerable hand on his head, and said, 'I believe God will raise him up for some remarkable work. I hope he will one day fill Rowland Hill's pulpit' It appears to me," continues the grandfather, "as if he spake under a spirit of prophecy. When Mr. Knill first heard of my grandson being in town, he wrote to me for his address. The reason he gave was, being then from home, with a large party of friends, after dinner, the conversation turned upon a wonderful preacher who was pastor of the New Park-street chapel. Mr. Knill inquired his name, and the answer given was—' Mr. Spurgeon.' 'I know him.' said Mr. Knill. 'No, no,' replied his friend, 'I think not.' 'Yes, I do, sir,' returned Mr. Knill. 'I saw him at his grandfather's house some years ago, when I preached in the village for the missionary cause, and have always been convinced that he would one day be a most extraordinary character in the Christian world. I remember,' continued Mr. Knill, 'taking the lad into the garden; I conversed with him, and prayed with him, and found that he possessed a mind far beyond his years.'"

Mr. Knill died at Chester three months ago, and was buried in the cemetery there; the greater part of the citizens showed their respect to his memory by attending his funeral; while among the mourners near the grave was the present Bishop of Chester, Dr. Graham. Here, then, we have very striking testimony to prove, that, very early in life, Mr. Spurgeon manifested those evidences of future usefulness and distinction, which have been so amply and so remarkably realized.

There is a power and influence in home training, which is capable of immense good or evil, according to the manner and direction given to the mind of a youth. As a rule, praying parents, if they make prayer a cheerful duty with their offspring, may have praying children. Mr. Spurgeon had the advantage of praying parents and grandparents. Chiefly to his beloved mother is he indebted for the bias of his mind toward the Word of God and the people of God. On every suitable occasion, his mother retired with him (and others of her children) into the quietude of the closet, where, by reading the Scriptures, and applying them to the spiritual wants of her child in the way many pious mothers have before done, and then praying with and for him, the love of these Christian duties grew with his growth, and prayer, and the study of the Bible, soon became his delight. Such exercises always strengthen affection between the members of a family, and similar results were experienced in this case. Between the child and his parents, on the one hand, and between the parents and the child on the other hand, as well as among the children themselves, there always existed the warmest possible attachment and affection. Happy children in praying families often sing—

> "When brethren all in one agree,
> Who knows the joys of unity?"

There still exist among all the members of the family the strongest feelings of personal concern and affectionate regard. Such maternal solicitude resulted in giving a decided choice to religion to the mind of her son Charles. So there is scarcely a period in his existence in which his mind has not been under the hallowing influences of personal, practical religion. "Seek ye first the kingdom of heaven," and God has declared himself engaged on the side of such seekers, to promote their Welfare every way.

When but a youth, scarcely in his teens, we learn from communications kindly furnished by Mr. Spurgeon's father, that the youth was often found in the hayrack, or the manger, reading aloud, talking, or sometimes preaching to his brothers and sisters, so anxious was he to be doing good. Such exercises encouraged the feelings, which were early manifested in favor of the ministry as the occupation of his life. And when he was residing at Cambridge in 1850, the entrance of one of his early companions on a collegiate course led his own mind in that direction for a time. In a letter written home to his mother at that time, he declines the distinction of joining his friend at college, and adds,

> "If the Lord will teach me to know his statutes, and prepare me to preach his gospel to his poor people, I have my desire. How happy is that man who spends his whole life in serving God, and can go to the heathen bearing the word of life. He is the noblest of all men."

These are the sentiments of a youth, deliberately written, at the age of sixteen.

In matters of religion, he was always before his age, and the teacher of his companions. While his brothers and other associates were engaged with amusements, and trifles, and mimic imitations of workmen, Charles H. Spurgeon eschewed all such pursuits, and taking his Bible, or other good book, would seclude himself, and with intense delight would study and read away the hours other children gave to play. He has never exercised himself in any kind of handicraft—the bent of his mind being entirely in another direction. He was a boy of strong passions, and always possessed a determined will. This gave great concern at one time to his parents, and most earnestly did they both pray that the great Head of the Church would give the lad grace to keep that will "under," and subject to the will of God. Both his parents had a firm conviction, which was confirmed by others who knew him, that he would one day occupy a distinguished place in the world, and hence arose their natural anxiety that their son should excel in the service of God.

Besides his strong passions and determined will, there were other points that had their influence in the formation of his character. From the earliest dawn of reason, owing to the care taken in his religious instruction, he appears to have had very clear views of the great leading doctrines of the New Testament. Of the condition of man as a sinner, and of the nature of the sacrifice and death of Christ, he was able to give a simple explanation as a child. Supported by a memory of great vigor and power, anything once learned was his own, and was never lost. Hence his preaching at the present time derives much of its efficacy and attractiveness from his great power of memory, furnishing always, at the right time, the right kind of illustration to make an argument clear to his audience, or to adapt things of the past to his present emergencies. Such a power of memory, and such an uninterrupted flow of language, suitable to every subject on which he may preach, seldom falls to the inheritance of ordinary men. Another important help in forming character aright Mr. Spurgeon has found in his simple habits of living, which have resulted in securing and fostering a healthy condition of both mind and body. He may be considered, on this account, capable of enduring an amount of labor and fatigue, which would destroy a frame more habituated to indulgencies. He knew not what illness was until the Surrey Gardens calamity, joined with the wicked calumnies of a portion of the press, laid prostrate even the strong man.

He had the advantage of an education in the best school that could be found; and if that education was not completed in a college, the fault was entirely his own. Often, and earnestly, was this point urged upon him by his parents; and on one of his father's visits to him while at Cambridge, he spent some hours in the attempt to convince his son of the advantages which such a course of study would secure to him; but in vain, as we have said on a previous page. He had a conviction on his own mind that his duty lay, not in a college, but in the church, and in the pulpit; and very many young divines have wasted years of precious time and energy in the cloisters of learning, which might have been better employed in the more active exercises of ministerial life. He did not conclude, however, against a course of instruction in a college without much prayerful deliberation, and the advice of those in whose welfare his heart's affections were bound up. He was already the pastor over a flourishing church when this subject came before him for consideration; and in a letter to his father, from Cambridge, in the spring of 1852, he writes: "I am not asking that I may not go at all [to college], but only that I may not go just now. The tears of the people I hope will prevail." And as he hoped, so God's providence decided; himself submissive to do that which his best friends in the church might, in answer to much earnest prayer, recommend. It is not the wisdom of man, nor the powerful influence of learning, but the "foolishness of preaching" which the Almighty owns in reaching and impressing the hearts of sinners.

Having received the instruction in Colchester which the best school could supply, when about fifteen years old, it was deemed expedient that he should have some knowledge of a few branches of learning which were specially taught in an agricultural college at Maidstone, then conducted by one of his relatives. There, however, he was left much to his own inclination, and he very eagerly devoted his leisure time to the diligent pursuit of such studies as were most congenial to his own mind. At Maidstone, as well as at the school at Colchester, he was the successful prize-man at the examination. Indeed, he never failed in gaining a prize at school on any occasion when they were given for success in study.

After remaining one year at Maidstone, he moved, in his sixteenth year, 1849, to New Market, where he was engaged as an usher in the school of Mr. Swindell. Mr. Swindell was a Baptist. At New Market, he pursued the study of the Greek and French languages, with great care and diligence. While he was eminently "diligent in business," he was equally "fervent in spirit, serving the Lord." His duties and trials in the school were such as would have broken down any but the most patient person. During the year spent at that place, many important changes had their origin, or their full development, which have greatly contributed to the remarkable success of our Southwark divine. There he learned to practice much self-denial. There, also, he began to see himself to be a lost and unworthy sinner, deserving the full punishment of God's anger upon his sins. There it was that he started on that "mad voyage," to which he has thus pathetically referred in one of his sermons.

Speaking of a free-thinker, he remarks,

> "I, too, have been like him. There was an evil hour in which I slipped the anchor of my faith; I cut the cable of my belief; I no longer moored myself hard by the coasts of Revelation; I

> allowed my vessel to drift before the wind. I said to reason, 'Be thou my captain,' I said to my own brain, 'Be thou my rudder,' and I started on my mad voyage. Thank God, it is all over now. But I will tell you its brief history. It was one hurried sailing over the tempestuous ocean of free thought." The result was that, from doubting some things, he came to question everything, even his own existence. Thus, "the devil foileth himself." Faith came to the rescue of bewildered reason, and, from that perilous voyage, brought back the wanderer "safe to land." She who had nursed him in infancy, like the grandmother of Timothy, is pictured as exclaiming before the throne of God in heaven, " I thank Thee, O thou ever-gracious One, that he who was my child on earth, has now become *Thy* child in light!"

There, too, having conquered those violent extremes to which Satan often drives the sinner who is repenting of his sins, and having fled for refuge, and found a welcome and safety in the bosom of a crucified Jesus, his sins forgiven, and his spirit enjoying the liberty of the adopted children of God, his joy knew no bounds. Although his life had been from infancy more or less devoted to the service of God, still he had not realized that change of heart, which is implied by the new birth. Under a powerful and impressive sermon preached from Isaiah 45:22, "Look unto me, and be ye saved, all the ends of the earth," the Spirit of God so wrought upon his heart, that after suffering much agony of mind, he found in believing that peace, which passes understanding. His spirit was now overflowing with happiness. All the letters he sent home at that period were full of the overflowing of a grateful heart. And although not sixteen years old, he describes the operations of grace on the heart and life, and the differences between the doctrines of the gospel, and the forms of the church, in terms so precise and clear, that no merely human power could have enabled him to do.

Being justified by faith, he had peace with God through our Lord Jesus Christ. He was taught experimentally, by the Holy Spirit—"... and spake unto him, and took of the spirit that *was* upon him" (Num. 11:25). He had hitherto been brought up among the Independents. There, and at that period, it was that his views changed respecting a point in church discipline. He had experienced a change of heart. He felt it to be laid upon him as an imperative duty to make a full and public confession of the change, by public baptism. He wrote many letters of inquiry soliciting advice and information from his father. On both sides, there was much frank and open candor. No arguments Mr. John Spurgeon, the Independent minister, could use, were considered by his soul as sufficient to alter his purpose of making a public confession of his faith in the manner named. At length, the father consents; the son satisfies his father clearly that he has no faith in baptismal regeneration; and the necessary steps are taken for his admission as a member into the Baptist church. In his last letter to his father on the subject, dated New Market, May 1, Mr. Spurgeon thus writes:

> "If I know my own heart, I believe that the sentiment uppermost there is, that salvation is not of man; that no works, however holy, can contribute in the least to save my soul; that the work is all of God's sovereign, electing love; and if ever I am saved, it will be by his power alone."

The necessary arrangements having been made, he walked from New Market to Isleham, seven miles, on May 2, and staying with the family of the Baptist minister there, Mr. Cantlow, he was publicly baptized in that village, by the minister just named, on Friday, May 3, 1850, being in his sixteenth year. He thus proceeds in the letter to his father before quoted from:

> "It is very pleasing to me, that the day on which I shall openly profess the name of Jesus, is my mother's birthday. May it be to both of us a foretaste of many glorious and happy days yet to come."

Who that has a heart to feel, would not heartily respond to such a prayer by such a son—AMEN!

Having thus publicly devoted himself to the service of God, he was more earnest than ever in his efforts to do good. Besides having himself revived an old society for distributing tracts, he undertook to thoroughly carry out this good work in the town. Whenever he walked out, he carried these messengers of mercy with him, was instant in season, and indeed was seldom out of season, in his efforts to do good. His duties in school occupied him three hours daily, the remainder of his time being spent in his closet or in some work of mercy. The Sunday school very soon gained his attention, and his addresses to the children were so full of love and instruction, that the children carried the good tidings home to their parents, and soon they came to hear the addresses in the vestry of the Independent chapel in that town. The place was soon filled. On Saturday, he had more leisure, and on that day, he commenced a new tract district in what is called the new town. During all that year, he was subject to personal trials, hardships, and inconveniences, which greatly exercised his faith and would have overwhelmed many, but he yielded not.

At one of the examinations of the school, it was his duty to deliver an oration on missions. It was a public occasion, and in the company was a clergyman. During the examination, the clergyman heard of the death of his gardener, and suddenly left for home; but on his way, thus reasoned with himself: The gardener is dead. I cannot restore his life—I will return and hear what the young usher has to say on missions. He returned, heard the oration and was pleased to show his approval by presenting Mr. Spurgeon with a sovereign.

While he was resident at New Market, Mr. Morley, of Nottingham, offered a prize for the best essay on Popery. Only three essays were sent in, one of which was written by Mr. Spurgeon. The Rev. George Smith, of Poplar, was the adjudicator, who, after a delay of two years, wrote a kind and encouraging letter to Mr. Spurgeon, stating, that his paper was not deemed entitled to the premium; yet the gentleman who offered it, and who was a relative, in approval of his zeal, and in the hope that he might employ his talents for the public good, sent him a handsome sum of money as a gratuity. This essay is entitled, *Antichrist and her Brood; or, Popery Unmasked*, and is thus endorsed—"Written by a boy under sixteen years of age." This early production of Mr. Spurgeon's pen has not yet been published.

After a residence of one year, he removed to Cambridge, and became usher under Mr. Henry Leeding, who had shortly before opened a school for young gentlemen in that university borough. Gratitude to Mr. Leeding for the instruction received from him at Colchester led Mr. Spurgeon to that establishment. There, his duties were less arduous, and his comforts greatly increased. He maintained his faith in God unmoved, though often it was tested.

The experience of most Christian churches goes far to prove that, with many young persons who become members, they find it expedient to identify themselves with a community of the people of God. With Mr. Spurgeon, religion was a matter of the heart—it was a principle. Go where he might, because his heart had been touched with a "live coal," from off the altar of heaven, he carried his religion with him; it was to be seen in his conduct, because it was a matter of experience within him. It was not merely a business, which could be put on or laid aside like a garment, but was the result of a deliberate and prayerful choice, proceeding from a course of careful training in "wisdom's ways." It was an emanation from the divine mind, with the will of the human nature yielding and consenting. God called; man obeyed. Truly happy are all who yield to the strivings of the Holy Spirit. A decided love of "whatsoever things are of good report" had been manifested in his life even from infancy.

When a child of very tender years, he strongly evinced his love of and preference to good people, and there are many aged Christians in the county of Essex who remember him as a child, with a countenance beaming with joy and delight, at having an opportunity of conversing with them on matters of personal religion. Of this number, there are not a few, faithful men of God whose daily privilege it is to pray for their young friend, that his life may be spared, and that his labors may be abundantly owned by a large ingathering of stray sheep into the fold of Christ. Out of many instances, which might be recorded in confirmation of this point of character, the following is given, just as it is furnished by Mr. Spurgeon's grandfather:

> "When my grandson was very young, he went one day into a field where a very pious man was plowing. He was a member of my church. The child began to ask some questions on religious subjects, which the good man thought far beyond his age. The conversation continued some time on spiritual subjects, until the man was quite amazed at what he had heard, although he was a man deeply experienced in the things of God. At last, the man said to my grandson, 'My dear boy, God has given you great gifts, great grace and great experience. My prayer to God for

> you is that he may keep you truly humble, for if you rise one inch above the ground, you must be cut down.'" Adds the Rev. James Spurgeon, "I cannot but hope that this prayer has been answered. I am amazed, and thankful to God, that my grandson is kept humble."

From such testimony, we learn this truly gratifying lesson—that God can perfect praise out of the mouth of "babes"—and that our young Timothy has "known the Scriptures" from a child. Unlike too many young professors, Mr. Spurgeon carried his religion about with him; and on removing to a large town, where many dangers were likely to beset his path, he at once identified himself with the people of God. How many there are who have to trace their declension in religion to a want of courage to avow themselves members of a Christian church, when they remove to a place where they are unknown. In London, there is a great multitude who thus suffer themselves to be robbed of the greatest blessings we can know on earth—even the communion of saints. In London, every denomination of Christians is so well represented, that no excuse can exist for young Christians, fresh from the country, not joining that form of religion in which they may have been brought up. Like a true servant of the Most High, our young friend could not be unfaithful to the vows he had taken upon himself. He had been useful in the Sunday school in giving practical and animating addresses to both children and their parents; he had been useful in visiting the poor at their dwellings, and carrying with him a little tract to instruct the ignorant, and being called of God to this work, he did it "with his might." He removed from New Market to Cambridge in the year 1850, after staying only one year at the former place.

Having at once identified himself as a member of the Baptist church in Cambridge, he soon found occupation suitable to his mind. His addresses to children, and afterward to parents and children, had produced a love of the work, and he soon was called to exhort a village congregation. He was then about sixteen years old. His duties in Mr. Leeding's school being lighter than in his former place, he had leisure to occupy himself in trying to do good. Connected with the Baptist church, meeting in St. Andrew's-street Cambridge (formerly under the pastoral care of the late learned Robert Hall), there existed a society entitled The Lay Preacher's Association. Although so young in years, Mr. Spurgeon was accepted as a member of this association. Here, he at once found the occupation, which his mind most desired, and he was soon appointed to address a congregation. Although we have not been able to learn what was the text selected by the youthful divine on this interesting occasion, nor have we heard any report of the service, we do know one result, which has proceeded there from. Good was done, and the preacher was encouraged. Mr. Spurgeon's first sermon was preached in a cottage, in the village of Teversham, about four miles from Cambridge. The Lay Preacher's Association was instituted to enable the poor inhabitants of the villages surrounding Cambridge to hear the gospel in their own homes, where dress would be no barrier to their assembling together, and at the same time, to provide them with preachers who should address them in terms, which they might readily understand. There were thirteen village stations mapped out, some of which were many miles from the town, and in one or more of these stations, service was held every evening in the week. Having once entered on this most solemn duty, and finding acceptance with the people, he laid himself out for one service every evening, after attending to his duties in school during the day. It would be unfair to criticize those early efforts at public teaching by the ordinary rules, which we apply to public preaching. The tender years of the speaker, and being besides self-taught in divinity, and in most of the branches of human learning, these should induce a spirit of forbearance. The desire and the ability to preach, God had implanted within him. Experience could only be learned by the exercise of the gifts, which had been bestowed. The New Testament teaches that both the operations of nature and of grace are progressive—that we have "first the blade, then the ear, after that the full corn in the ear" (Mark 4:28). These early preaching efforts were acceptable to the people, and they were owned and blessed by God. From an aged and experienced Christian who heard Mr. Spurgeon preach before his call to London, we learn that his addresses were very instructive, and often included illustrations derived from history, geography, astronomy, and from other branches of school occupation, evidently adapted from his daily duties, and thus made to serve as instruments in religion as well as in training and informing the mind. Since Mr. Spurgeon has been the popular preacher of the day, we have often heard mammon-getting men of the world ascribe his popularity to motives so mercenary that we will not betray the ignorance of our fellow-citizens by repeating them. They have gone beyond the point of impugning the preacher's motives, and have censured his deacons as participators in the results we have referred to, and prompters to a course of action as base as can well be attributed to fallen human nature. All such notions are as groundless as they are uncharitable, and as unreasonable as they are untrue. For several years, Mr. Spurgeon had no gain whatever from his benevolent labors, but hopes of many kinds. Even at the present time, though he is the almoner of the bounty of many, and the generous bestower of his own goods to feed the poor, he has neither the riches nor the influence, which are often ascribed to him. Few public men are paid worse than public preachers for benevolent objects. The early ministry of Mr. Spurgeon was not only gratuitous, but also often attended with demands on his small salary, which he willingly gave to God not to be seen of men, but to help the needy. The poor man's preacher, in all ages of the church, has always been poor, and though the bounty of others may make him the dispenser of their wealth, he cannot himself preach the everlasting gospel and amass riches for his reward. From the commencement of Mr. Spurgeon's ministry, it may be truly said, "the common people heard him gladly." From the first, the result has been the same in two respects, his hearers have been uniformly numerous, and his preaching as uniformly acceptable. The motives, which impelled his choice, justify the result. He has often said in effect,

> "The love of Christ doth me constrain,
> To seek the wandering souls of men."

This had been the earnest desire and prayer of his parents for many years. Anxiously did they pray that their son Charles might be a servant of Christ and a preacher of righteousness. On one of his visits home, he was told by his mother that she had thus prayed for him, but she added that she had never prayed for him to be a Baptist. The ready mind of her son at once replied,

> "Then, mother, God has answered your prayer and, like his bounty, has given you more than you asked."

It will be remembered that both his grandfather and his father are ministers in the Independent body. There is a command addressed thus to all children—"Obey your parents in all things." Mr. Spurgeon was long in correspondence with his father in reference to this change in his religious profession and, like a dutiful son as he had always been, he did not give up his connection with the Independents until he had obtained the free and full consent of his father to do so. A son who is obedient to his parents will also obey God. Would that the example of this young man had been followed by many who have professedly given up the religion of their fathers, and have become perverts to the heresies of Rome. Had they first assigned their reasons to their parents, and asked their counsel and consent, there might have been no Cardinal Archbishop now in England, allured here by the false idea of the heart of the people leaning toward Rome. God loves obedience, and He will as assuredly punish those who are guilty of the opposite sin as he punished the disobedient prophet, or Saul, the first king of Israel. Children, young men, Sunday school teachers, learn a lesson from this young man: although his reason was convinced and his judgment persuaded, still he yielded not to either until he had complied with the command of God—"Children, obey your parents."

In some of the thirteen village-stations around Cambridge and Waterbeach, to which Mr. Spurgeon devoted all his evenings, the preaching was held in a cottage, in others in a chapel, and occasionally the open air alone could furnish the accommodation required. Some of these chapels belonged to the Independents, others to the Wesleyans or the Baptists, and members of each denomination flocked in large numbers to hear the "boy preacher."

At the village of Waterbeach, Mr. Spurgeon was received in a marked manner of approval. In most of the places in which he had preached, the effect was very much alike in the large numbers attracted to hear the Word of God, and in the success, which God was pleased to bestow on his labors. Even at that early period of his ministerial career, invitations to preach special sermons in towns and villages at a distance soon rapidly increased. At Waterbeach, however, the little church saw in the young man a suitability to their wants, and they gave him an invitation to become their pastor. The building used as a chapel there was formerly a barn with a high-pitched roof, which is covered with thatch. The walls are a conglomerate, although made to look neat and clean by a plentiful coating of whitewash. It is an edifice, which is sure to attract the attention of the passer-by. The following engraving is from a sketch recently made by Mr. E. Bowman of Castle End, Cambridge, for this work.

We quote the following notice of the young pastor of the Baptist church at Waterbeach, from a communication kindly furnished by Mr. C. King, one of the deacons of the church:

> "From Mr. Spurgeon's first coming to Waterbeach, he was generally well received, and soon became quite popular as a preacher. It was not unusual to see the laborers on the farms at a distance from the village literally running home when the duties of the day were over, that they might be in time to attend his ministry in the evening. At the early age of eighteen, he was unanimously chosen pastor of our little church. We have often sat under his ministry with a mixture of pleasure, profit, and surprise, and have been ready to exclaim with the inquiring Jews named in the Gospel, 'Whence hath this young man this wisdom and these mighty words?' Our congregation soon rapidly increased, so that both the seats and the aisles were generally filled, and some could not obtain admission into the place. A reformation in the habits of the people soon appeared in the village and about twenty persons were, in a short time, added to the church. Mr. Spurgeon's character and conduct were as amiable as his talents were attractive; and when, after preaching for some months on the Sabbath morning and afternoon, he was met by the request to preach on Sabbath evenings also. He modestly replied, 'I cannot always preach three times, for I am not so strong a man!' After having labored among us upward

> of two years, in season and out of season, he was called to a wider sphere and left us, to the general regret of the church and congregation; and he is followed by the prayers and best wishes of the little flock he had partly gathered out of the world, and left behind."

Waterbeach is a village of about 1,300 inhabitants, scattered over a considerable surface, the occupation being agricultural. The Baptist church there numbered nearly forty members when Mr. Spurgeon was called to the pastorate. During the short period of his ministrations there, the number of church members was doubled. It must be remembered that the income of the pastor over so small a church was only a nominal sum. For his maintenance, he had still to pursue his daily duties as usher in the school at Cambridge, for three hours in the morning, and in the evening, the young preacher was addressing a congregation of villagers. Not only at Waterbeach, but also at all the villages he visited, there was a spirit of inquiry among the people, of "What must we do to be saved?" God's Holy Spirit awakened and answered that inquiry. All religious meetings were well attended. The Lord was exalting himself by calling some of the vilest of the people to forsake their evil ways, and become regular attendants on the worship of God. The whole village was reformed.

During his pastorate at Waterbeach, in the year 1852, his father again opened the correspondence respecting his going to college, generously offering to make any sacrifice to secure such training for his son as would be afforded by that course of study. In his reply to his father, dated March 9, 1852, he writes:

> "I have all along had an aversion to college; and nothing but a feeling that I must not consult myself but Jesus, could have made me think of it."

After confirming his views expressed in a former letter on the same subject, he proceeds:

> "It appears to my friends here that it is my duty to remain with my dear people at Waterbeach; so say the church there unanimously, and so say three of our deacons at Cambridge."

In another letter to his excellent mother, dated November, he confirms his former decision thus:

> "I am more and more glad that I never went to college. God sends such sunshine on my path, such smiles of grace, that I cannot regret if I have forfeited all my prospects for it. I am conscious I held back from love to God and His cause; and I had rather be poor in his service than rich in my own. I have all that heart can wish for; yea, God giveth more than my desire. My congregation is as great and loving as ever. During all the time I have been at Waterbeach, I have had a different house for my home every day. [His residence was at Cambridge.] Fifty-two families have thus taken me in, and I have still six other invitations not yet accepted. Talk about the people not caring for me, because they give me so little, I dare tell anybody under heaven, 'tis false! they do all they can. Our anniversary passed off grandly; six were baptized; crowds on crowds stood by the river; the chapel afterward was crammed both to the tea and the sermon."

By these and like exercises, God was preparing this young divine for greater plans of usefulness, and a wider sphere of action. The Holy Spirit had called him to His work, and he believed in the same divine power for the qualifications necessary for the duty he was to fulfill. Mr. Spurgeon had strong faith, and he exercised it: the result has, by God's blessing, justified his choice. Strong in the conviction that the pulpit, not the college, was his place, he maintained his point, and the issue has proved the soundness of his judgment. He continued to reside at Cambridge during the week, merely spending the Sabbath and an occasional evening at Waterbeach. During these visits, the homes of the villagers were his welcome; and with one after another did this evangelist abide for a Sabbath day, until he had been invited into nearly every homestead in the place. His usefulness so greatly increased his duties, that he found it requisite to leave Cambridge, and go to reside altogether at Waterbeach, during the summer of the year 1853.

Having by his earnestness, usefulness, and diligence, obtained great favor and acceptance among the people of God in Cambridgeshire and Essex, his fame spread rapidly in all directions. Besides visiting many poor and sick persons, and administering comfort and consolation to them, he had to travel many miles to the various villages; and during the year before his residing entirely at Waterbeach, he preached more than 360 sermons and on nearly every occasion to overflowing audiences. Such unceasing and heavy duties in the cause of the Great Master of assemblies, in no way lessened his zeal or his love to the work.

Living in constant personal communion with heaven, he had a motive for being earnest, which mere hirelings in the Lord's vineyard do not possess. He saw much good being done continually, and knew it was of God, and not of man. Because he was a faithful servant, he found a faithful Master, and thought no duty too heavy to do for so good a Master.

CALL TO NEW PARK-STREET

The Cambridge Union of Sunday Schools is a very efficient institution. Its anniversary meeting in 1853 was held at Cambridge, on which occasion Mr. Spurgeon was called upon to speak. Whether as a preacher in the pulpit, or a speaker on the platform, he can always command the attention of vast multitudes. It is not, however, on the platform that Mr. Spurgeon is most at home. He can move a resolution with marvelous effect; but he prefers preaching for any good object rather than advocating it in a set speech. As a speaker, he succeeds; as a preacher, he excels. The part he took at the anniversary meeting referred to, was of remarkable significance. There was nothing in his manner or his remarks that was especially attractive to the audience; but there was an unseen agency at work with the speaker, as well as in the audience. Great and important issues often proceed from small beginnings. There was present at that meeting, a young man from Loughton, in Essex. Mr. Spurgeon's address made an impression of lasting importance upon his mind. Shortly afterward, the young man met with one of the deacons of a Baptist church in London, which had once flourished like the cedars of Lebanon, but which was now, although improving somewhat in condition, so far shorn of its former glory as to furnish cause of serious consideration. Anxiously did the thoughtful deacon relate his tale of a scattered church and a diminished congregation to his Christian brother from the provinces. Nor was this unreasonable, considering the untaught multitude around their chapel, the unlit sittings and impoverished funds. Fresh upon the mind of the young man was the effect of the speech of the youthful Timothy at Cambridge, and he ventured to speak of the evangelist of Waterbeach as a minister likely to be the means of reviving interest in the church at New Park-street. The friends separated: the deacon left, unimpressed by what he had heard, and things grew worse. God's ways are not as our ways.

> "A wonderful fashion of teaching he hath;"

and while he deviseth, he will execute. It was not likely the church, which had been raised by a Keach, and supported and extended so widely by a Gill and a Rippon, should thus decline without hope of recovery. When a man's extremity is greatest, then the Almighty graciously assists. Shortly afterward, the deacon and the Essex friend met again; and again was the young preacher of Waterbeach recommended as the means of reviving the once prosperous church of "Hors-lie-down." Seeing that some change must be made, the good deacon thought there might be some hope in at least considering, and naming to other friends, what he heard. No sooner had the intelligence reached a second and a third member of the church, than they resolved upon action, and soon forwarded an invitation to the young man to come to London and preach before them in their large London chapel. The work was of God; man only made the arrangements. What Julius Caesar said of himself may be appropriately said of Mr. Spurgeon: He came—he preached—he conquered. The provincial brother suggests, and the citizens accept. In autumn 1853, Mr. Spurgeon was first invited to occupy a London pulpit. He was then just nineteen years of age, but having been trained by the best Teacher, in the best kind of knowledge, and feeling assurance in the efficacy of his message, he delivered his first sermon in New Park-street chapel on a Sunday morning to a small audience, with the freedom and boldness that evinced that he believed what he preached, and believed that his message was from God. Some were disappointed; others resolved to oppose, and did oppose; but by far the greater proportion were disposed to hear him again. The result of the first sermon was proved, in a few hours, to have been a success. The evening congregation was greatly increased, partly from curiosity, partly from the age of the preacher and his unusual style of address. We have before remarked how much the early sermons of Mr. Spurgeon were illustrated by scholastic knowledge; astronomy, history, geography and other like subjects being made to serve his purpose. This was the case on the present occasion. Having served the church on one Sunday as a temporary supply, he was again invited to take the pulpit on another Sunday as early as possible, for a feeling of excitement was created, and it required being satisfied. After consulting with his church at Waterbeach, he arranged to supply the Park-street pulpit during three alternate weeks, coming to London on Saturday, doing full duty on Sunday, and after another service on Monday evening, he returned to his charge in the country on Tuesday. The six weeks having expired, and the excitement in the neighborhood to hear the young preacher having become considerable, it was determined to invite Mr. Spurgeon from his rustic retreat, to undertake the heavy responsibility of pastor of one of the most ancient, and formerly the most influential Baptist church in London.

The stone cast in the water produces a succession of circles, which expand beyond control. The ripple on the ocean's brink may be small in itself, but it is the indicator of a power, which is omnipotent: it shows the direction of the current. It will be seen, by reference to preceding pages, that for nearly 120 years, the church of New Park-street had been presided over by only two pastors, both of whom were called to the pastorate while very young. Here then was the prestige of example to justify the choice of the church in appointing Mr. Spurgeon their pastor. Such was the depressed condition of all the funds of the church, that there was no pecuniary inducement whatsoever to entice the popular preacher. Nor has this motive ever been chargeable on Mr. Spurgeon since he has been in the ministry. He has always been content with, and thankful for, whatever the circumstances of the church afforded. As a teacher, his financial prospects would have been much brighter; as a preacher, he had not hitherto received a fair compensation for his untiring and earnest labors. But the call to London opened up to him a much wider prospect of doing good: he thanked God, and entered on the duty in the month of January 1854.

He had not long officiated in Southwark before the chapel began to fill, and applications for sittings rapidly increased. The tidings of his preaching spread from friend to friend, and almost from house to house in the neighborhood until the place was filled to overflowing. Many who had been members, but who had strayed, now returned to their old church, and great fear was freely expressed in some neighboring congregations, lest the members should leave to go and hear and sit under the young divine. Every fresh accession, to either the church or congregation, served to increase the excitement, and large numbers were often unable to get within either the chapel or the school-room. The following description of the preacher's style at this period is one of the earliest we have met with:

> "His voice is clear and musical; his language plain; his style flowing, yet terse; his method lucid and orderly; his matter sound and suitable; his tone and spirit cordial; his remarks always pithy and pungent, sometimes familiar and colloquial, yet never light or coarse, much less profane. Judging from a single sermon, we

supposed that he would become a plain, faithful, forcible, and affectionate preacher of the gospel in the form called Calvinistic; and our judgment was the more favorable, because, while there was solidity beyond his years, we detected little of the wild luxuriance naturally characteristic of very young preachers." Want of order and arrangement was a fault the preacher soon found out himself, and refers to it when he says: "Once I put all my knowledge together in glorious confusion; but now I have a shelf in my head for everything, and whatever I read or hear, I know where to stow it away for use at the proper time."

Among the weekly multitudes that assembled to hear the now popular preacher, after he was established at New Park-street, was a member of the Society of Friends who, being deeply impressed by what he saw and heard, wrote a lengthened article on the subject, which was published in *The Friend*. A few extracts from this account, by an unprejudiced observer, will very appropriately supply reliable information respecting Mr. Spurgeon at that early period of his ministry in London.

The Friend says:

"An extraordinary sensation has recently been produced in London by the preaching of a young Baptist minister named C.H. Spurgeon. The crowds, which have been drawn to hear him, the interest excited by his ministry, and the conflicting opinions expressed in reference to his qualifications and usefulness, have been altogether without parallel in modern times. What renders the present case remarkable is the juvenility of the preacher—his hold on the public being established before he had attained his twentieth year; and his first appearance in London being that of a country youth, without any of the supposed advantages of a college education or ordinary ministerial training.

> "Early in 1854, he undertook the charge of the congregation assembling in New Park-street chapel, Southwark. It was a remarkable sight to see this round-faced country youth thus placed in a position of such solemn and arduous responsibility, yet addressing himself to the fulfillment of its onerous duties with a gravity, self-possession and vigor that proved him well fitted to the task he had assumed. In a few weeks, the pews which had been so long tenantless were crowded, every sitting in the chapel was let, and ere many months had elapsed, the eagerness to hear him had become so great, that every standing-place within the chapel walls was occupied on each succeeding Sabbath, and it became evident that increased accommodation must be provided for the wants of the congregation. It was about this period, in the autumn of 1854, that we first heard C.H. Spurgeon, on the occasion of his preaching at the Young Men's Christian Association. The preliminary portions of the service were conducted in a manner at once to impress the hearer with a sense of the earnest reverence, which the young pastor felt in his work. He read a portion of Scripture, accompanying it with a few forcible and pointed expository remarks, these expository efforts being of peculiar value to the class of hearers of which his congregations are mostly composed. His sermon was a deeply impressive one. He spoke as a young man to young men, sympathizing in their tastes, their trials, their temptations and their wants. He unfolded the plan of salvation, and urged the importance of a manly and decided profession of Christianity."

These extracts are sufficient to show that there is something in Mr. Spurgeon more than ordinary, to secure for him in his public ministrations such crowds of attentive hearers. Nor was it alone in his chapel that these multitudes of people gathered to hear him. He was employed almost every day in preaching for some benevolent object, either in London or its suburbs, or in some provincial town or village; and on every occasion, he not only led a large audience, but the largest, in most cases, which had ever assembled at such services.

During the autumn of the first year, 1854, many who were unable to go and hear Mr. Spurgeon for themselves, formed an estimate of the young divine by his sermons, several of which were published at short intervals. These met with such a ready sale that by the end of the year, Mr. Joseph Passmore, a relative of the late Dr. Rippon and an intimate, personal friend of Mr. Spurgeon, commenced a publication entitled, *The New Park-street Pulpit*, containing sermons preached and revised by the Rev. C.H. Spurgeon. It may be desirable to add, "No sermons are genuine reports unless they bear the title, *The New Park-street Pulpit*, or the names of Alabaster & Passmore, and of those issued in America the imprint of Sheldon, Blakeman & Co." These sermons have from the first been sold at one penny weekly; and being the only authorized sermons of Mr. Spurgeon, the demand for them has so far exceeded the supply as at first published, that all the early sermons have reached a second edition, and some of the later ones also. At the present time, the demand for these sermons is increasing weekly; and taking into account the regular weekly issue during the past two years, there cannot be less than half a million of Mr. Spurgeon's sermons in circulation at the present time in Great Britain. Nor is it in England alone that these sermons are so much desired.

It was at this period—the autumn of 1854—that the faith, patience, courage and zeal of Mr. Spurgeon were tested in a remarkable manner. Already he was popular, among the poor particularly. There was then raging over Europe one of the scourges of the world—cholera. Almost without intermission, by night and by day, the presence of the New Park-street pastor was entreated by the suffering and the dying. So great was his faith in God, that young though he was, he went wheresoever he was summoned; and during its continuance, so many were the cases he visited, read to, prayed and conversed with, that the recital of those scenes would be something appalling. He toiled until his physical energies were well-nigh exhausted; and when, on one occasion, having that day witnessed some half dozen of these terrible deaths, he was again hurried from home to witness the same distressing agonies repeated, his heart almost yielded to rest. He went out mournfully contemplating, when, seeing a scrap of paper wafered on a shop window, curiosity led him to read the words written upon it. They were: "Thou shalt not be afraid for the terror by night; *nor* for the arrow *that* flieth by day; *Nor* for the pestilence *that* walketh in darkness; *nor* for the destruction *that* wasteth at noonday" (Psalm 91:5-6). God's servant was reassured; his faith was confirmed; and thus, Providence helped when help was most required.

The popularity of Mr. Spurgeon had so far increased his audience on the Sabbath day at New Park-street and inconvenienced the members of the church that the chapel became far too small for the weekly requirements, and before the year 1854 had passed, the deacons resolved to enlarge the chapel. While this change was in progress, Mr. Spurgeon's members and friends met every Sunday for worship in Exeter Hall, in the Strand. Here arose one of the many problems, which has been proposed by the press and the public concerning this young man, "Will Mr. Spurgeon fill Exeter Hall?" Some doubted, but the solution in this case was speedily achieved. The first time Mr. Spurgeon preached in the large room, Exeter Hall, was on Sunday morning, February 11, 1855. Truly, it was an imposing sight to see such a large audience gathered, from every part of London, to hear a sermon by a young man but lately fresh from the country. The large hall was filled in every part, and so great was the desire to join in these services, that often during the four months required for enlarging the chapel, the crowds were far greater than the hall could accommodate. The hall was occupied during the months of February, March, April and May; the last service was on May 27. The chapel in New Park-street having had the northern end wall removed, several yards were added to the length of the building, which afforded sittings for nearly 300 additional persons. After the re-opening of the chapel, with all the new sitings taken, and numerous applications for sittings being still unsatisfied, the deacons were obliged to content themselves with having provided as much room as the space would afford, and all who could not gain admission were obliged to leave the place. The number thus disappointed every Sunday amounted to hundreds, often to thousands.

His ministrations continued with unabated interest and with astonishing success during the year 1855, which was his second as a London pastor: twice on Sunday in his own tabernacle in Southwark, and again on Monday and Thursday evenings, with a chapel filled on each occasion; while during the intervening days, we see his name in the public papers constantly, advocating as a preacher the cause of some religious society. Thus, the benevolence of his heart is taxed, as much as the energies of his body and mind, in trying to benefit mankind on a large scale. One very remarkable feature of Mr. Spurgeon's popularity is that it knows no variation or diminution. Does he occupy his own pulpit, either on Sunday, or on a week day, the place is always full. Is he in the suburbs, or in the provinces, on any day in the week, whether in the morning, afternoon, or evening, the place is full, and often the assembly outside is greater in numbers than those within the building, and not infrequently an address has been delivered to the congregation outside by some other minister.

Seasons of special blessings should be recognized by Christians as occasions for special acknowledgment and thanksgiving. The Jews are remarkable for their strict observance of their annual festivals and their jubilees. In the summer of this year, 1855, Mr. Spurgeon completed his twenty-first year. This festive occasion was commemorated by a sermon, which Mr. Spurgeon preached in his own chapel, to a very large audience, which was published, and has since passed through several editions, under the title of *Pictures of Life, and Birth-day Reflections.*

Mr. Spurgeon spent the greater part of the month of July in the north of England. During his travels and preaching engagements among the Scotch, an impression was made upon the mind of the inhabitants for good, which will live after many days. In the city of Glasgow, which was his headquarters, he visited all the buildings and places of note. Like the great Apostle Paul when at Athens, his spirit was moved within him, and he gave free vent to his feelings. Of one of his rambles, he writes:

> "One feels all his hatred of popery revived when he finds himself on the eminence of the Necropolis, by the base of Knox's monument. There he stands, stern as Elijah, rough as the Baptist, and earnest as Luther. The statue is well placed on a hill overlooking the cathedral, so that the fine structure seems to lie at his feet, and he appears to view with complacency the house he had so thoroughly purged."

On Sunday, the fifteenth, Mr. Spurgeon preached to perhaps the largest audiences ever gathered to hear the gospel in that city; in the morning, in Dr. Patterson's Baptist chapel, Hope-street, the largest in Glasgow; and in the evening, to a multitude in Dr. Wardlaw's Independent chapel, West George-street. Mr. Spurgeon was received with great suspicion in Scotland. "At the close of each of these services," observes Mr. Spurgeon,

> "I learned the meaning of the text, 'So then, we are no longer strangers and foreigners;' for I found that the children of God recognized the herald of truth, and cheerfully gave me their hearts and hands."

He proceeded northward to Perth, Dunkeld and Aberfeldy. Of this journey, Mr. Spurgeon writes:

> "If anything in our island could raise the feelings of a man toward heaven, surely the sight of the scenery of Scotland might suffice to do it. For my own part, when viewing the rocks of Aberfeldy, I could not refrain from clapping my hands for very joy at such a noble display of my Father's power, and my heart leaped at the thought that the Captain had provided such a magnificent resting place for his warriors."

While at this romantic village, the bellman was thrice sent round to announce a sermon by a minister from the south, in these words:

> "Your auld playmate, and auld acquaintance, Shony Carstair, wants to see you all at the Independent chapel at 7 o'clock to hear my dear friend, the Rev. C.H. Spurgeon, preach."

Here followed an account of the crowds who had flocked to hear the preacher at Exeter Hall, and concluded thus:

> "Mind, he has come 500 miles to tell you something for your good, and the Rev. C.H. Spurgeon and I expect you all to come and give us a hearty shake hands."

Such an unusual mode of announcing a sermon was sure of success—the whole village was moved, and though the preacher, during the service, "tried all means to move them," the cold blood of the men far north was undisturbed by Mr. Spurgeon's appeals, and the only movement seen in the congregation was a free use of the snuff box, the men "using a small spoon to shovel the snuff from the box to the nose!" The sermon over, before the benediction was pronounced, a rush was made simultaneously, and ere the preacher could descend from the pulpit, the chapel was deserted! Such is a glance at Mr. Spurgeon's day spent at Aberfeldy, and of a Highland congregation.

Returning home from the north, Mr. Spurgeon preached at Bradford, in St. George's Hall. On Sunday, July 13, he had addressed multitudes in Glasgow; on July 22, the locality is changed, and so is the scene. The Scotch character is but little susceptible of those emotions, which, in a more southerly temperature, spread from mind to mind, enkindling warmth as they spread. The largest edifice in that populous town was engaged for the use of Mr. Spurgeon. Admission was by ticket, and days before the services, the tickets were selling at a premium. On the Sunday morning, hours before the service, all the roads leading to the town were thronged with eager pilgrims journeying to hear this evangelist from the south. One of the thousands who were unable to gain admission into that vast hall has described to us his astonishment at seeing such multitudes, old and young, rich and poor, the merchant and the weaver, all gathering to one spot to hear the gospel. The whole town was in commotion. The morning sermon was preached from the address of Pilate to the Jews, "Behold the Man!" In the evening, the scene was one that defies description. Although 5,000 persons were crowded into the hall both morning and evening, there were assembled in the evening outside the hall, unable to gain admission, fully 5,000 persons more. The sum of £150 was collected at these services on behalf of three of the Sunday schools in Bradford.

Immediately on his return from the north, we find the active mind of the New Park-street pastor anxiously and earnestly engaged in the work of ameliorating the condition of the poor around the chapel. In the district of St. Peter's, Southwark, in which Park-street is situated, there are more than 3,000 children under 14 years of age. For these, there is Sabbath-school accommodation for only 800, and day-schools for only 360. In order partially to remedy this sad state of things, a number of gentlemen connected with New Park-street chapel were formed into a committee to establish a mission hall, reading- and school-rooms, under the direction of the Rev. C.H. Spurgeon. A trip to Rosherville, on August 7, first brought this proposal prominently before the church and the public. Half the sum required for the work was realized by that trip. At a public meeting held on November 9, the remainder of the sum of £250 was obtained to enable the committee to establish the mission hall and schools. Premises were at once taken in Guildford-street, on a lease for 21 years; an active missionary was appointed to visit every family in the district; and on October 29, 1855, the new premises were opened by a prayer-meeting, after which 150 children were admitted into the day-school, 100 of whom had never before been in any school. The reading-room, and the lectures given therein, has been a great blessing to many poor families in the district. The first anniversary meeting was held in January 1857, at which a very encouraging and satisfactory account was given of the working of the school during the year.

About the end of the summer, 1855, a younger brother of Mr. Spurgeon, the Rev. James A. Spurgeon, then about seventeen years of age, who is still a student in the Baptist College, Regent's Park, commenced his pulpit ministrations in London with much acceptance. Owing to the unparalleled popularity of the elder brother at New Park-street, Mr. James Spurgeon often had to supply the appointments made by his brother. He has met with a welcome in the churches where he has preached, which bespeaks for him a respectable place among the uprising divines of our own times. Two of the sermons preached by the Rev. James A. Spurgeon have been published, one of which has met with public favor, the second having been just published, and entitled *Peter's Danger and Peter's Safety.*

Early in September, Mr. Spurgeon gathered around him in a field at Hackney, a concourse of about 12,000 persons, to whom he delivered a sermon of extraordinary power and pathos, which was soon published, and entitled *Heaven and Hell.* So greatly was that vast multitude influenced for good by the sermon that its publication was required, and it has had a sale of nearly 10,000 copies.

In the autumn of 1855, we find the public papers of the west of England for several weeks full of accounts of the immense gatherings of people, and the extraordinary sermons of Mr. Spurgeon, in the two great cities of the west, namely, Bath and Bristol. Early in the month of October, he had undergone the toils of a preaching tour in the east of England, starting from his old rendezvous, Waterbeach, and passing through Cambridgeshire and Suffolk, preaching daily, and sometimes twice or thrice. On October 30, he preached at Ebenezer chapel, Bath, and in Castle Green chapel, Bristol. On the next evening, the large Broadmead Rooms were taken by storm by an eager audience, and a thousand citizens stood outside in that wide thoroughfare, unable to enter, but determined to listen. On this occasion, Mr. Spurgeon introduced the story of Jack the Huckster in his sermon, with an effect for good, which will last for many days. On the morning of November 1, Arly chapel was crowded by citizens of the upper class. By this time, the city was in a commotion with the preaching of the young Baptist minister from London. The last of the Bristol services was held in the chapel of good old sainted Winter, at Counterslip, on the next morning. Here, high and low, rich and poor, were gathered together, and in that audience were two, at the least, professed unbelievers—infidels—upon whose minds the Holy Spirit of God wrought with such power, by means of that sermon, that they abandoned their false principles, and became converts to the truth of Christianity.

With the opening of the new year, we find Mr. Spurgeon entering on a new and changed condition. For several months previously, many strange statements had been in circulation respecting presents made by ladies to Mr. Spurgeon, which had no foundation in truth. The marriage of this popular minister had been a subject of very frequent remark, and public opinion had selected many partners for the young pastor. But Mr. Spurgeon made his own choice, and was married on Tuesday, January 8, 1856, to Miss Susannah, daughter of Mr. Robert Thompson, of Falcon Square, London. This event was to the happy pair a religious service, and not, as is too often the case, looked upon merely as a civil contract. On that auspicious morning, New Park-street chapel was filled to excess, and some 2,000 persons remained outside unable to gain admission. Dr. Fletcher, of Finsbury chapel, commenced the service at 11 o'clock, by giving out the well-known hymn, "Salvation! O the joyful sound!" The doctor then read the 100th Psalm, and then offered up a solemn and affecting prayer. A short and appropriate address followed. The form of marriage used by Protestant Dissenters was then gone through, and after Dr. Fletcher had pronounced them man and wife, part of Ephesians v. was read, and the wedding hymn sung, commencing, "Since Jesus freely did appear." Dr. Fletcher again implored a blessing on the happy pair, who, having left the chapel, the assembly separated. The bride and bridegroom were both attended by their parents. We have thus detailed an outline of a Christian marriage; it may serve as a model worthy the imitation of many Christians, and particularly of Christian ministers.

After a brief sojourn on the continent, we find Mr. Spurgeon in a synagogue of the Jews; remembering the example of the great Teacher who, before his ascension, commissioned his disciples to preach the gospel to every creature. He manifested his love to the Jews by adding to that commission "beginning at Jerusalem." Christ loved the Jews, although they crucified him; and Mr. Spurgeon, in his written account of the Jewish synagogue of Duke-street, after describing the service and his introduction to and conversation with Dr. Adler, the chief rabbi, observes:

> "We must express our intense love for the Jews, and earnestly hope that the church of Jesus will arouse itself to a more determined effort for the conversion of this ancient race."

On March 14, Mr. Spurgeon preached to a large audience in the Hanover Square Rooms, on behalf of the Exeter Buildings' Ragged School. This sermon has since been published under the title of *A Visit to Calvary*, in the second series of sermons issued by Sheldon, Blakeman & Co.

Early in April, Mr. Spurgeon delivered a lecture on the Study of Theology, before the Young Men's Christian Association at Newington. The lecture abounded with various practical illustrations, and in it, the lecturer stated, that his own method of breaking up hard texts of Scripture was to consult first the best commentaries at his command, and if they failed, he took his Bible and offered this prayer:

> "O Lord! teach me what this means;" and, "It is marvelous," observes Mr. Spurgeon, "how a hard, flinty text struck out sparks with the steel of prayer."

On Good Friday, in 1856 and in 1857, Mr. Spurgeon preached to very large audiences in Cambridge. During the same month, April, again he made a preaching tour to the west of England, extending to Brighton, and over part of the eastern counties. At Trowbridge, the multitude was so great at the evening congregation, that in consideration of the large numbers who were unable either to see or hear the preacher, Mr. Spurgeon, after a little refreshment, preached again to the disappointed people at 10 o'clock at night.

About the same period, a momentous controversy was pervading every religious community in England, arising out of a few pages of rhyming nonsense, published by the Rev. T.T. Lynch. The point in dispute was "Neology," or Rationalism from Germany. In May, Mr. Spurgeon published *Mine Opinion* on this volume, and a more withering exposure of dangerous theology and bad poetry we do not remember to have met with.

During the month of June, we find Mr. Spurgeon preaching one day in Exeter Hall; on another, to a multitude who had to adjourn from a chapel into an orchard; the day following, to a mixed multitude in a large barn. Next, he is surrounded by an immense assembly in the Bunyan Meeting at Bedford; then at the Beaumont

Institution, Mile End, and he closes the month's journeying by a week's sojourn and preaching at Bristol and Clifton, preaching usually twelve sermons weekly.

We find him in July 1856, attracting immense multitudes to his ministry in various parts of Scotland; he next takes the sedate city of Oxford by surprise, of which visit the *Oxford Chronicle* says: "Few of the immense audience who were privileged to listen to his pulpit ministrations here but were astonished and delighted at the wonderful power and ability with which Mr. Spurgeon is so highly gifted."

Mr. Spurgeon commenced the month of September by preaching in Dr. Fletcher's chapel, Finsbury; on the following day, in St. Martin's Hall, Long Acre, he preached a very remarkable sermon, entitled "Seest thou this woman?" on behalf of the London Female Dormitory. On September 16, he preached two sermons in Luton, and a local journal, in recording this visit, informs its readers that these special services of Mr. Spurgeon are purely gratuitous, as he never charges more, and sometimes less, than his traveling expenses. This statement we not only can confirm, but can add, that during the past year, Mr. Spurgeon has himself stated that he sustained a loss of £25 by these preaching tours; for when he preached for his poorer brother pastors, he usually declined to receive any contribution whatsoever toward his personal outlay.

At the end of the month of September, a great meeting was held in New Park-street chapel to adopt measures for the erection of a large tabernacle. After describing the utter inadequacy of the chapel to accommodate the thousands who assembled every week to hear the minister, Mr. Spurgeon observed,

> "he came to the determination to become an itinerant evangelist, if a place were not erected of a size more commensurate with

> the extraordinary congregations who flocked to hear him. He confessed that it gave him great pain to see people who had come long distances having to stand during the whole of the services, while large numbers could not enter the building, yet remained to hear stray sentences, and crowds went away without being able to get even within hearing."

Mr. Spurgeon further observed,

> "They had an accession of 500 communicants in little more than two years, who had given credible testimony of having been the subjects of conversion."

Mr. Deacon Moore confirmed the remarks of their pastor, and added,

> "From thirty to forty communicants were added to their church every month, till they now, as a church, numbered nearly 900 members."

It was finally determined that no steps be taken toward the erection, or the selection of a site, until the expiration of twelve months, during which period the friends are to exert their energies in obtaining contributions. It is expected that $60,000 will be required, and it is proposed that the new tabernacle shall accommodate 5,000 persons.

Owing to the multitude of people who flocked every Sunday to hear Mr. Spurgeon in Exeter Hall, which was always filled to overflowing, it became necessary to find another capacious edifice when Exeter Hall was no longer available. The deacons of New Park-street chapel next entered into an arrangement with the proprietors of the Royal Surrey Music Hall for the use of that building once at least on the Sunday, for which the sum of £60 was to be paid for four Sundays. The first service was commenced on Sunday evening, October 19, when some 14,000 persons assembled in the hall. From some cause, which is not satisfactorily accounted for to this day, an alarming excitement was created at one corner of the building, which soon spread throughout the vast audience, and in consequence, several persons lost their lives and many were injured. After an investigation by the coroner, which extended over several days, the jury returned a verdict of accidental death with regard to those who had lost their lives. No one suffered more from this sad event than the pastor himself did. So heavy was the blow upon his nervous system, that had he not been at once removed into the country, it is very doubtful whether he would have been again in a condition to preach. Mr. Spurgeon had enjoyed good health during the whole of his previous life, but this event completely prostrated all the energies of a strong man. On Sunday morning, November 2, though far from well, he again appeared in the midst of his beloved people at the Surrey Gardens, and was received with every manifestation of joy.

November, last year, 1856, was one hundred years since George Whitefield opened the Tottenham Court Road Tabernacle. The centenary services were held in that month, and Mr. Spurgeon preached the third of the sermons from the prayer of Habakkuk, "O Lord, revive thy work." It is computed that the building would hold 4,000 persons; but a much larger number were packed within its walls on that occasion. Such a crowd probably has not been seen in the building during the present century. Since the services we have just noticed, an unfortunate fire has left this fine and memorable edifice a heap of blackened ruins; nothing but the external walls remain.

The desire to hear Mr. Spurgeon at the Music Hall during the present year, 1857, has been on the constant increase. Nor is the excitement confined to the lower or middle classes of society. One of the earliest men of mark who attended to hear Mr. Spurgeon, was the Lord Chief Justice of England, Lord Campbell, who met there on that occasion, Sir Richard Mayne, chief commissioner of police, to whom his lordship remarked, after the service, "He is doing great good, sir, great good." The Lord Mayor and Sheriffs, Lord John and Lady Russell, Lord Alfred Paget, Lord Panmure, the Earl of Shaftesbury, Earl Grey, the Bishop of London, Sir James Graham, the Duchess of Sutherland, the Earl of Carlisle, the Earl of Elgin, Baron Bramwell, Miss Florence Nightingale, Dr. Livingston, Lady Lionel Rothschild, and many other distinguished persons have since formed part of Mr. Spurgeon's audience. What is it attracts all these persons from time to time to hear the youthful divine? There is a cause—who will declare it?

Early in the present year, 1857, there appeared the second volume of the *New Park-street Pulpit,* containing fifty-three sermons, preached and revised by the Rev. C.H. Spurgeon. This volume contains the principal sermons preached by Mr. Spurgeon during the year 1856, and the most of these are contained in the second series published by Sheldon, Blakeman & Co. Not the least useful and remarkable of the sermons in that volume is the last one, entitled, "Turn or Burn!" and with those solemn and impressive words, the volume is closed. It would be invidious to particularize any of those sermons, but some of them have been made especially useful in arresting sinners and in stopping them in their career of wickedness.

A penny sermon of Mr. Spurgeon's was made instrumental in the hands of God, in stopping an infidel of some renown in Norwich, in his career of unbelief and sin; and so deeply was the man's mind impressed with the truth of divine revelation by reading that sermon, that he took all his infidel publications and publicly burned them in the cattle-market in that city. So fierce has been the persecution, which the secularists of Norwich and Norfolk have poured on the head of this valiant champion of truth, that he has been obliged to remove to another town, to secure to himself and family the peace of a home where Christ reigns. Only a few weeks ago, while on our way from the country on Sabbath morning to the Music Hall, Mr. Spurgeon was the subject of conversation in the railway, when a gentleman observed,

> "For seventeen years I have been an infidel; but hearing that young man preach a few times, my unbelief has fled, and I have now no greater delight than in attending on the ministry of the young man who has been the means, in the hands of God, of totally altering my religious views, my habits and manner of life."

Besides a numerous class of persons who have voluntarily supplied information of the benefit they have personally derived from reading these sermons, there are others who, in secluded places, far removed from church or chapel, having become acquainted with these sermons, now obtain a regular weekly supply; and on the Sabbath, the inmates of two or three cottages assemble and read them as they appear. Not a few farmers have supplied themselves with a volume, and on every Sabbath evening, the servants unite with the family in domestic worship, and a sermon of Mr. Spurgeon's always closes the service. Quite recently, a gentleman in Sunderland obtained a few of Mr. Spurgeon's sermons, and on Sunday morning, a large number of working men assembled in a public room to hear one of the sermons read. The audience was so delighted, that a large supply was demanded, and the gentleman was requested to continue the service. Not only in these private assemblies is good being done by Mr. Spurgeon's published sermons, but in other places, more publicly, is the good work being carried on. Clergymen and ministers of various denominations send for large assortments of these discourses, and, not in a few cases, by inquiry, we have ascertained that Mr. Spurgeon's sermons are delivered to more than one public congregation, and often in consecrated edifices, on the Sabbath day. "Who shall measure the amount of good, which is being thus done daily, in every part of the country, by these penny weekly sermons?

One of the most widely circulated religious newspapers in England, and one conducted with great ability, says of this extraordinary man and his preaching:

> "Mr. Spurgeon is unquestionably a phenomenon; a star, a meteor, or at all events something strange and dazzling in the horizon of the 'religious world.' The old lights have gone down, and since Irving, and Hall, and Chalmers 'fell asleep,' there has been no preacher that has created a 'sensation' at all to be compared with the young preacher at New Park-street chapel. But do not let our readers imagine that they have found here a luminary of the same class with those we have just named. Whatever Mr. Spurgeon's merits may be—and he has some rare ones—they are of a very different order from those that distinguished the mighty preachers of the last generation. They were all men of gigantic reasoning powers, of refined taste, of profound scholarship and of vast theological learning. Of all these qualities, Mr. Spurgeon has little enough; nor, to do him justice, does he pretend to any of them, except perhaps in some unlucky moments to the last. But it will probably be agreed to by all competent judges, that neither Irving, nor Hall, nor even Chalmers, was so well fitted to carry the gospel to the poor and

ignorant, as is this modern orator of the pulpit. Their writings will last for many generations, and will be as fresh to the latest as they are today; Mr. Spurgeon's sermons will, perhaps, soon be forgotten forever, but they go to the hearts of the multitude; and as he has the good sense to know the direction in which his talent lies, he promises to be incomparably useful in a class of society, which preachers too often complain is utterly beyond their reach.

"A lively imagination, sometimes rising to the region of poetry, but more frequently delighting in homely and familiar figures of speech; a free colloquial manner of address, that goes directly to the understanding of the simplest; and an enthusiastic ardor, that may prove catching to all his hearers, unless they are more than usually insensible, are the chief legitimate attractions of Mr. Spurgeon's style; and they are qualities so rare in their combination, and are in him so strongly developed, as to stamp him, in our judgment, with the decided impress of genius. We should suppose that it must be impossible to hear him without acquiring for him a sentiment of respect; for if offended by his extravagances, as the thoughtful certainly will be, the offense is so immediately atoned for by some genuine outburst of feeling, that you remember that his extravagances are but the errors of a youth, and that the material on which these excrescences appear is that out of which apostles and martyrs have in every age been fashioned. You pardon his follies, for they are nothing else, for the sake of his unquestionable sincerity and impassioned zeal. You wish that it had been possible that a mind so gifted might have received more culture before it was called into its present dangerous position; but finding it as it is, you accept it with gratitude, and pray God, the All-wise, to be its guide and protector."

And an American newspaper of a denomination to which Mr. Spurgeon does not belong, bears the following noble testimony to the power and goodness joined in this remarkable preacher:

> "Effects prove a cause. Where results are undeniable, reasons for such results must exist. When, then, we find men thronging in thousands, month after month, to hear the preaching of the plainest truths of the gospel by a young man of twenty-three, with nothing external to himself to clothe him with popularity, we may rest assured that there is a cause for the fact. Having received from the publishers a volume of the sermons of Spurgeon, the London celebrity, we opened it, with a desire to search for a clue to his extraordinary popularity. This we did, not from mere curiosity, but in the belief that our ministry might find profit from the study of the sources of his power, wherever they might lie.
>
> "We are free to confess that we have been agreeably disappointed in these sermons. There is in them more to praise and less to condemn than we had been led to suppose by current reports and descriptions. They by no means so abound in frothy declamations, extravagancies and coarse wit, as many may suppose; nor can the popularity of the preacher be attributed to these sources of attraction for the populace. On the contrary, these sermons contain the evidences of a real power and effectiveness in the highest sense. They are well worthy of the study of those who long for an increase of influence over the hearts of men.
>
> "His style is in many respects admirable. It is English—not Latin, not Greek, not French, but English—the language, not of Coleridge, nor of Johnson, but of the Bible and of Bunyan—not of the metaphysician and theologian, but of the farmer,

the mechanic and the laboring man—in short, the language of common life, the language understood, spoken and appreciated by nine-tenths of the people. Here is one of his strong points. We have in these days too much preaching for the parlor, and too little for the kitchen. Our pastors speak rather to the most than to the least learned in their flock. Spurgeon speaks to the common people in their own tongue, and the common people hear him gladly. Yet he is not vulgar as to style—every page shows that the Bible and the hymn-book are the two fountains from which he draws his greatest store of literary wealth, and we know of no two sources so valuable; the Scripture-text and the verse of sacred song always command attention. These Spurgeon constantly uses. He evidently has them at his tongue's end.

"His mental characteristics stand out boldly: imagination lively and uncultivated, at times defective, native mother-wit frequently more than verging on coarseness or profanity, fine descriptive powers, with intense earnestness. Take the first sermon in the series, 'God our glorious Habitation.' Commencing in simple style, he leads you to the wilderness to stand with Moses on the rock, or points you with lively imagination to the people passing through the arid wastes of the desert; his wit keeps you awake; his descriptions and illustrations preserve a lively state of attention; his hymns and Scriptural quotations touch and improve; and his earnestness drives home the whole with the power of a great reality upon the hearer.

"The pulpit, in refined communities, is in danger of being emasculated by a care for the proprieties, of being frozen by dignity, and petrified by conventionalism. Rowland Hill-like, Spurgeon dares to meet the people on their own level, and they, in return, flock to meet him. He does not befog them with

> 'objective' and 'subjective' views of subjects, or put them to sleep with well-rounded periods, or weave fine-spun webs of philosophic network, in which to envelop a plain truth—but he gives them the truth as plainly as God has given it to him; rough at times, it is true, but we can excuse roughness in cannon-balls, and flaws in the sword that cleaves through helmet and mail.
>
> "Spurgeon is thoroughly in earnest. His theology is a positive one, a tough, old-fashioned Calvinism, and he seems to believe it and to feel it. He appears to have, what of all things is the most essential to a preacher, an individual religious experience. He feels strongly, and he speaks strongly; nor is he afraid to let the people know that he believes for himself what he commends to them. If we may judge a man by his words, this young man communes with his Bible, and through it with God, and gets his power thence. We see no great evidence of the study of theology, but we do see evidence of the study of God's Word—we see deep conviction of the reality of heaven and hell—we see a hearty, open, earnest utterance of this belief enforced by all the abilities, which God has given him, and we do not wonder that Spurgeon is popular."

Such is the testimony that pours in upon the publishers of these sermons from every quarter in England and America. Wherever the English language is spoken, they are read with instruction and joy, and fruit is borne to the glory and praise of God.

One of the most eminent Presbyterian divines, himself distinguished for the learning and grace with which he adorns the pulpit, has expressed the wish that there were a hundred Spurgeons in London and fifty in New York, at this moment. What a power, what a glory would such an army with the banners of salvation produce! Who can estimate the effect that would be wrought if only a score of such men should stand in our halls and churches from Sabbath to Sabbath proclaiming, with burning words, the everlasting gospel of Christ! In saying this, we make no reflection upon the able and excellent men whose ministry it pleases God so largely to bless at the present time. It is not in the order of his Providence to raise up men like Spurgeon often. They come, like angels' visits—few and far between; but when they do come, they are to be hailed as special messengers of mercy, to call sinners to repentance. Such a man was Whitefield, and God was honored in his labors, his life and his death; and there are hundreds now in heaven praising God for the gift of "that seraphic man," who turned many to righteousness, and now shines as a star in the firmament. Such a man was Summerfield, whose sun went down in the morning; but he left behind him a memory, fragrant as the most precious ointment, in the church of God.

Spurgeon is not a whit behind either of these men in graphic power, while he is vastly superior to them in logic and illustration. He grapples with the strongest truths, unfolds the profoundest doctrines, plies the lever with the stoutest arguments and aims at convincing before he attempts to persuade. He has, therefore, all the elements of great usefulness and of permanent popularity.

The reception of his sermons in the United States of America has no parallel in the history of this department of religious literature. Without any of those aids to popularity that they have in England, where the voice of the young living preacher has been heard all over the land, and thousands will try to read the eloquence that has thrilled their hearts. Here no one has heard his voice, but these printed pages have come with messages of salvation, and have been hailed with joyful emotion by thousands in all parts of this vast country. Up to this date, 44,000 volumes have been sold, and it is less than a year since the first was published. Twenty-five thousand of these volumes have been sold within the last twelve weeks, and orders are flowing in for them so rapidly that a thousand copies per week will not supply the demand. This is the more remarkable, as it occurs at a time when there is comparatively little demand for books, and the trade is languishing. The publishers receive daily from the clergy of all evangelical denominations, the most valuable and hearty assurances that the sermons of Mr. Spurgeon are just what they and their people need and love. Churches that are destitute of pastors have called for these sermons that they may be read from the vacant pulpit. And it may be safely said that ***hundreds of thousands*** in this western world have already been brought under the power of the truth as preached by this youthful herald of the cross.

One of the most extraordinary facts remains to be mentioned: the secular press in the United States, with unexampled unanimity, has commended these sermons: their boldness and directness, their glowing eloquence and great ability to command the respect and admiration of all cultivated men.

From the various reviews in the magazines and quarterlies, we take the following from the *Christian Review*, as a fair analysis of Mr. Spurgeon's manner, style and secret of the power with which his sermons are pervaded.

SPURGEON AS A PREACHER

It is a fact in the history of pulpit oratory, which ought no longer to be blinked, that the sermons, which have most powerfully moved the common mind, have always, been marked by certain peculiarities of matter, language and illustration. Different from each other they are, in many lesser points, but in the main features they all bear a general family resemblance, which distinguishes them from the mass of discourses, which are composed by learned and experienced pastors, and intended to edify the pious of their flocks, or to lead to the cross the unbelievers of their congregations. Before hearing Mr. Spurgeon, we had come to some conclusions as to the general nature of his eloquence, apart from the special attraction of his delivery, his youth and his personal appearance—apart from the piety of the preacher, and the zeal, spirituality and cooperation of his flock—apart, also, from the gracious co-working of the divine Spirit, whose all-powerful agency is, on no account to be ignored, in any fair estimate of the cause of ministerial success. Waiving for the present the statement of these conclusions, it is sufficient here to say that we were fully confirmed in them when we heard the young preacher on various occasions, and under circumstances that were likely to call out all his powers, and display them in an advantageous light.

As you stand among the crowd at his chapel, waiting to enter, you see a young man to whom all give way, as he lifts his hat and bows along his path to the vestry. Many who stand in the outer edge of the throng are glad to catch even a glimpse of the young preacher, as they have but a faint hope of gaining a place where they can hear him. They see so much good nature in his face, and so much civility and heartiness in his manners, that they are more eager than before to listen to the sound of his voice. They are sure that he does not think himself holier than other good people, or lifted by his honors above the poorest of London's poor. Upon taking your seat in a crowded pew, you observe none of that profound silence, which usually reigns where a congregation of strangers is merely waiting to hear some great, but unknown, preacher. The kind and cordial deacons in white cravats are very busy giving a place to this comer, and promising one to that, presently. From the seat behind, you overhear two young converts talking anxiously in an undertone, about a young friend, for whose conversion they say they are praying, and they hope that Mr. Spurgeon may have a message for his poor soul tonight. Soon every voice is hushed, and all eyes are turned toward the pulpit. In walks a young man, with an air of perfect abstraction. His erect attitude, and his slow and careful step, suggests to you the idea of a hollow man of glass, who could not be jostled in the least without spilling something, and which would be broken into a thousand pieces, were it by any accident to come in contact with the side of the pulpit. But the stateliness vanishes the moment he commences talking about the hymn that he is going to read. He evidently would banish all formality, without loss of time, and fasten the attention of his audience on the holy work they have come to do. The hymn being read, the entire congregation joins in the song with hearty and honest spirit. It is no mere feeble, "Quavering and semi-quavering care away." It is no plaintive air, sung by a choir, nor yet is it a solo executed by some leader of an operatic troupe. It is a plain, old, homely hymn, such as poor people carry about in their hearts and memories, repeat at the fireside, at the family altar and while plying their tasks;—such as the pious mother sings to her infant while rocking the cradle, and the plowboy sings to the gods of the winds, the birds and the brooks;—such as the godly craftsman sings to the timing of his tools, and the patient porter hums to his heavy tread, as he trudges along the smoky lane.

Then follow his readings and expositions of the Holy Word. His talent for exposition, which he regularly exercises, is truly extraordinary, and is no doubt enriched by considerable study. Without being nicely critical, his remarks are discriminating, and at the same time, pithy and practical. He excels in spiritualization, and in happy turns of devout thought, and sidewise views of familiar passages. His prayers are marked by fervor, simplicity and brevity. He gives a loose rein to his imagination in his prayers even more than in his sermons; and his utterances of adoration and praise are often truly sublime. His importunities and pleadings, especially for the aids of the Holy Spirit, are humble and earnest.

Mr. Spurgeon is a little below the common stature, with a person that inclines to the thick and plump. The color of his eyes is black, his hair dark chestnut, and his complexion is bloodless; his face is a medium between the circle and the square, and approaches either according to the point from which it is viewed. It is rather sleek and inexpressive, and as the lymphatic prevails in his temperament, it is in keeping with a spirit naturally cheerful and content. In his general figure, he does not promise to become a St. Bernard: tall, thin, delicate and fleshless. His joints are by no means firmly set; and he has a curious litheness of limb. One is at a loss to comprehend how the oily and the adipose could long keep the company of so firm, active and persevering a mind. His voice is full, clear and musical. It is not commonly raised above the conversational tone, and is never heard in vociferous bursts and fulminations. It is singularly adapted to the expression of the plaintive and the pathetic. He is not a rapid or fervent speaker, being never caught up and carried away with his subject, but rather keeping that firm footing whereby he is able to catch up and carry away his audience. His gestures are few and natural. When animated with high thoughts, he looks aloft, and has the rapt and enthusiastic air of Powers's new statue, *Il Pensoroso*; when his ideas are familiar, he stoops over the pulpit, rests on his elbow, and sometimes ungracefully places his breast on his open Bible. His general manner is serious, frank, and calm, yet tender and genial. He has more humor than wit, but little of either has yet ever appeared in his sermons, and it may admit of a doubt whether either has much share in his mental composition.

With such advantages of person and manner, he associates higher qualities, which he possesses in common with most of the great preachers, who have been the favorites of the people. One of the most conspicuous of these qualities is boldness. This young preacher's boldness manifests itself in various ways. We cannot concur with those who say that he is very impudent—though he may sometimes seem very impudent to those who do not consider that it is not optional with this lad whether he will only utter such truths as would adorn the modesty of a youth who has no higher call than that of talking in a parlor. He may also seem very impudent in the eyes of those pulpit orators of the metropolis whose audiences are thinned in numbers by his superior attractions, and very impudent to those senior laymen to whose ears the force of the naked truth is too painful. Still, it must be allowed that he has a moderate amount of impudence, which it is hoped that his growing graces will temper.

His boldness often shows itself in manliness and even nobleness of thought. Of all preachers, save Paul, Chrysostom has ever seemed to us most excellent in this regard. But he reserves it mainly for great themes and great occasions, whereas Spurgeon has a faculty of ennobling common and familiar subjects by taking high and extended views of them, or by having the courage to set a plain truth on a higher and more suitable pedestal that it was wont to occupy. He invests the work of saving souls from death with a godlike dignity; he restores to their place of moral grandeur, the miracles of Christian experience, and, without permitting the unregenerate man to pride himself on the impulses of his humanity, he teaches the poorest saint to glory in the riches of present grace and the hopes of heavenly glory. His boldness also assists him to maintain his independence. Many young preachers are enfeebled by officious advisers, or corrupted by persons of some consideration in the church, who imagine themselves to be, and would have the young pastor believe they really are, the makers and destroyers of clerical reputations. Their counsels are to be his law, their usages his precedents and their example his guide. Not infrequently, some old man sets himself up as dictator, and as the young man has not the hardihood to resist the authority of gray hairs, he dutifully places his hand into that of his blind and trembling guide, not considering that according to Solomon, "the hoary head is a crown of glory" only when it is "found in the way of righteousness;" and not considering that the young prophet who could resist the tempting offer of half a kingdom was turned aside into the way of destruction by the advice of "the old prophet." There are those who think Mr. Spurgeon very audacious in adopting as his motto, *Cedo nulli*, "I yield to none." But it seems to us that he would have been audacious if he had made the multitude of his counselors, or any one of them, the keeper of his conscience and of his reason, the regulators of his zeal, and the taskmasters who should assign him his field and his work. Advice would not be given as freely as it is, if it were prepared at any great cost of thought, and if the adviser were made personally responsible for the results in time, and at the last judgment.

Our preacher's boldness often takes the shape of frankness. Somebody has well defined eloquence to be simply speaking out—a definition that is especially applicable to the highest eloquence of the pulpit. The gospel is an inward light whose very nature it is to shine whether through the lips or in the life. The man of God is, or ought to be, so filled with the Spirit of all grace, and so habitually swayed by the principles of the gospel, that he has nothing to fear from flinging forth all his uppermost thoughts, and giving voice to his most transient emotions. And this he may do without bolting out what his reason and conscience forewarn him not to say; without uttering what is immodest, laughable and coarse; without that stick-at-nothing kind of impudence, which regards neither person, time, nor place. Mr. Spurgeon often betrays a positiveness and even dogmatism, which his boldness assists to sustain. He knows that cool and connected reasoning would be lost upon most of those who go to hear him, and that it is worse than in vain to argue plain questions with cavilers and skeptics; that as we correct the senses by reason, so we ought to correct reason by the heart; that, if he can first convince the conscience and move the affections, then reason will not only do its office better than before, but will not, as it is often to be feared it will, continue turning over the question and starting doubts about it, on purpose to keep the moral sense fast asleep.

Another quality that pervades his discourses is clearness, in the fullest sense of the word. When we consider that Mr. Spurgeon's themes conduct him down into the deepest mysteries of Christian experience, and aloft away into the clouds and darkness of the divine purposes and providence—that he stops not on the confines of this world, but penetrates far into the unlimited light of heaven, and the smoke and glare of hell—when we consider these things, along with the fact that his mind is naturally of the poetic order, it is surprising that his ideas should be couched in language so luminous and distinct, that the most ignorant and feebleminded of his flock could find no difficulty in comprehending them. We must hazard the assertion that no preacher of any note, in our language, is so great a master of the quality in question, if we except John Bunyan, who well understood its power as a means of moral aggression. In the *Holy War*, he mentions "Plain Truth Hill" as one of those mounds that were cast up outside the walls of Mansoul, and upon which were stationed slingers to throw stones into the beleaguered town. Most orators become verbose and obscure when they are seized with a grand or sublime thought; but this young preacher, in common with a few orators, such as Demosthenes, Chatham, and Robert Hall, has the rare power of expressing grand and sublime ideas in language the most simple and unambitious. He makes it his boast that, like Whitefield, he uses "market language," though in fact it is something quite superior to it. However, it is such plain and pure old English as brings him into full sympathy with the people, and enables him to exercise lordship over their hearts.

This preacher has formed one habit of mind, which affords him great assistance amid his crowded engagements. This is a habit of assimilation.

> "I can't make out,"

said a minister to him,

> "when you study, Brother Spurgeon. When do you make your sermons?"
>
> "O!"

he replied,

> "I am always studying—I am sucking in something from everything;—if you were to ask me home to dine with you, I should suck a sermon out of you!"

Most active is the process by which his intellect converts the fruits of his reading and observation into its own nature and substance. Let it be a striking fact in science, a curious work of art, or some rural scene, a popular saying or a poetic quotation, or an anecdote, or an event in history, or some classic myth, or Rabbinic legend—it is sure to pass to its place in the depths of his memory, there to await the fires of his heart to melt it into the common mass of discourse, and project it upon his audience. When you examine some of his discourses critically, you are reminded of those masses of lava, into which precious stones and pieces of gold have been kneaded by the action of subterraneous fires. Most speakers and writers possess this faculty, but few ply it with such burning earnestness as to melt finer substances into the original matter so completely that it is well nigh impossible to separate them. Let it not be supposed, however, that this habit of assimilation hangs as a clog upon his soaring genius, forbidding it to mount superior to all merely human sources of information. Those who judge these sermons by the rules laid down in our theological schools may perhaps say that some of them are second-rate, but they cannot say they are second-hand. We live at too late a day in the march of centuries for borrowed eloquence to make any great commotion, even in England, where it is most tolerated. When the real Jupiter thunders, he shakes the heavens and the earth; but when your mock Jupiter Salmoneus manufactures noise, he simply stuns my ears and shocks my nerves. While, therefore, his habit of assimilation does not diminish aught of his power to create, it is a source of that freshness and fruitfulness of thought for which his sermons are remarkable. He has revived that mode of treating religious subjects, which was pursued by most of the old Puritan preachers. Like them, he has not been ashamed to labor with a view to furnish the people with a variety of "things new and old." He has offered them, at the same time, something more delicious than they were accustomed to receive, more delicious because new to them, though in reality, it is older than that which they have generally regarded as the oldest. He has now supplied them with the "old corn of the land," after they had been fed forty years with the daily manna in the wilderness. The mass of modern church-goers are strangers to some of the better qualities of the old Puritan preachers and orators. They have seldom, if ever, tasted the sweetness, juiciness, and wholesomeness of Bunyan, Baxter, Flavel, Bishop Hall, Leighton, Gurnell, Thomas Brooks, Matthew Mead and Thomas Watson. Serious, quaint, and pedantic as these writers sometimes are, they nevertheless abound in luscious clusters of heavenly thought, in beautiful lessons of experience, and in a generous unction and thorough practicality, which came of long and varied afflictions, leisurely study, and devout meditations, duly combined with laborious activity in the care of poor and persecuted flocks. Mr. Spurgeon has deeply imbued his mind with the spirit of these old writers, and, without copying the style, or quoting much of the matter of any of them, he has been led by the reading of them up to the sources of their inspiration in the oracles of God. He has thus pursued a course, which will enable him to overtake, if not to go before them.

The pathos, which is another characteristic of Mr. Spurgeon's eloquence, is rather the result of his compassion for human woe, his power of personification, and his skill in the delineation of scenes in the life of the poor, than of any melting sensibility that is natural to him. Often bringing tears into many an eye, he hardly ever weeps himself. Indeed, he appears to be deficient in what the

Romanists ascribe to some of their saints—"the gift of tears." His neighbor, Rev. Gordon Hall, who occupies the pulpit of Rowland Hill, has far more sensibility than he does, but much less power to excite that of his congregation. So far from grief being necessary to excite grief in others, sheer dissimulation to woe may suffice:

"False tears true pity move."

Besides, there may be something in the subject itself, or in the occasion, or in the circumstances of the audience, to elicit a degree of feeling to which the speaker is a stranger. Our orator finds the true pathos in the scenes of common life, for they appeal to the sympathies of our common nature. The parable of the prodigal son touches all hearts, because all cherish affecting memories of father, brother, boyhood and home. And accordingly, our preacher tells, perhaps, of a mother's love for a wayward son; or her tenderness to a sick daughter; of the poor father's daily toil to keep his family from starving; or of some Magdalen's repentance and pardon. Perhaps he describes how some stouthearted father was bowed down by overhearing his little daughter praying for him, or how some wandering son is brought to his knees by the reading of an old letter, discolored with the tears of his now sainted mother. He is fully aware that he cannot come at the feelings of some except by a circuitous path. In his account of a preaching tour in Scotland, he says, "I knew that you must often enter the heart by ridicule. Tender hearts may be entered by pathos, but hard hearts must be touched by something telling and singular." These last must, in his opinion, be made to smile before they will weep. We must, however, avow ourselves to be of the number of those who doubt the necessity of raising a laugh before we can start a tear, and who doubt the genuineness of that pathos, which is obliged to resort to such means of attaining its object; for we know that the buffoon can make people weep through sheer excess of mirth. What are such tears worth? The debauchee can weep in the morning following the night of his revel, but are his tears those of a contrite spirit?

But our preacher is sometimes compelled to go back still further, in order to find his way to the hearts of the dull and untutored multitude. He must first arrest, and then hold their attention—difficulties of which those preachers who customarily address refined and educated congregations have little knowledge. In one of his sermons in Park-street chapel, Mr. Spurgeon said,

> "I am not very scrupulous about my manner of doing good. I told the people of Scotland, when they said I preached in such an extraordinary way that they really did not understand me, 'Why, bless your hearts! I would preach standing on my head if I thought I could convert your souls, rather than preach on my feet!'
>
> "Whitefield, Berridge, Rowland Hill and Cecil, occasionally resorted to tact and ingenuity to recall the vagrant thoughts of their congregations. It is a fact not generally known to classical scholars, that Demosthenes himself employed a little pleasant artifice to rebuke the inattention of the fickle Athenians. While he was one day speaking to them upon a state of political affairs, he observed that something had diverted them from what he was saying. Whereupon, he immediately broke off his argument, and told them that he had something special to relate, if they would lend their attention. The curiosity of all was awakened. "Two men," he said, "having bargained for an ass, were traveling from Athens to Megara on a very hot day. Both strove to walk in the shadow of the ass. One insisted that the other had hired the ass, and not his shadow, and the other maintained that he had

> hired the ass and his shadow, too." At this point, Demosthenes began to retire from the assembly, but the Athenians besought him, with vehement cries, to return and finish the story, when the orator reappeared and said, "O, ye Athenians, will ye attend when I speak to you of a shadow and an ass, and will ye not attend when I speak of the great interests of the state?"

It must not escape our consideration, that these sermons are thoroughly Biblical in doctrine. No undue prominence is given to a favorite dogma, and no argumentation is employed in its defense or promotion. Ever bold in confessing himself a staunch Calvinist, he devotes but little time or space to the direct furtherance of any one point of his cherished faith. Taking the ground that Calvinism long ago fought and won the battle, he conceives it to be his duty to sit down among the trophies of the victory, and arrange the articles of a safe and abiding peace with all poor, weaponless sinners. "It is my firm belief," he says, "that what is commonly called Calvinism, is neither more nor less than the good old gospel of the Puritans, the Martyrs, the Apostles, and of our Lord Jesus Christ." The doctrines, which have been of late most generally preached in England, are Arminianism and Rationalism; and inasmuch as they had obtained great popularity, it has been justly thought to be the sign of a mighty reaction in religious opinion, to find a man obtaining great fame by a bold preaching of what are called the Doctrines of Grace. And we cannot help believing that Mr. Spurgeon owes much of his success in winning souls to the cross, by his open and uncompromising declaration of the doctrines in question. Sir James Mackintosh has recorded an opinion on this subject, which is worth the most serious attention, coming, as it does, from a historian and a philosopher who stood aloof from every Christian persuasion, and, it is to be feared, from Christ himself. In his journal, he says:

> "The revival of religious zeal is indeed common to all Christian communions; and I found remarkable symptoms of it last year among the Jews in Holland. But I do not know how to explain what seems to be a pretty certain fact, that in proportion as it becomes ardent, it approaches more or less to a Calvinistic form."

To a mere philosopher, it might indeed seem strange, that a system, which ascribes so much to the divine sovereignty and grace, and whose practical workings seem to him to be intended to waste the energies of the soul in the barren contemplation of what was in the Infinite mind before the world was, and to paralyze all its moral powers by leading it to brood over its own helplessness—that such a system should, in its actual operation, rouse it to the most strenuous endeavors to obtain the free and unmerited gift of salvation.

Another ingredient of his excellence as a preacher is the directness of his applications. Like Massillon and Baxter, he makes frequent use of the pronouns "he, you, thee, and thou," and whenever you hear him, you feel that you are brought, not only in contact with the speaker, but with his subject as well. You feel that religion is not merely the great interest of mankind in general, but your own personal concern. His warm and frequent interrogatives also produce the same impression upon you. He is not careful to regard that cold rule of criticism, which forbids their use, except for the purpose of clinching an argument or urging a conclusion.

In nothing are modern sermons more deficient than in the length and closeness of the application. Mostly occupied with exposition, illustration, or discussion, they afford little space for "uses," and these are often vague and pointless. The Pharisees of eighteen centuries ago, or the Papists of distant Italy, would be warned and instructed very effectually were they present to hear; but unhappily, they are not present, and the Phariseeism and Romanism in the hearts and lives of those who are, could not be exposed without molesting much peaceable self-complacency and much comfortable good will. A great number of passages might be quoted from the sermons of Mr. Spurgeon, to prove that he has rebuked the worst sins of a corrupt capital, and urged considerations for abandoning them at the foot of the cross with moving earnestness and pointed and straightforward freedom.

The following passage will illustrate, in part, what we have just said with respect to his applications:

> "There was a feast once, such as, I think, scarcely ever was seen. Ten thousand lamps lit up the gorgeous halls; the king sat on his throne; and around him were his wives and concubines. They ate, they drank; the bowls were filled to the brim, and merrily the hours danced on. Loud was the bacchanalian shout, and loud the song. They drank deep, they drank curses to the God of Jacob; they took the sacred wine-cup, and they poured in their unhallowed liquors; they drank them down, and drank again, and the merry shout rang through the halls; the viol and harp were there, and the music sounded. List! List! list! it is the last feast that Babel shall ever see. Even now, the enemies are at the gates. They come! They come! O Belshazzar! read that writing there—'Thou art weighed in the balance, and art found wanting.' O Belshazzar! stay thy feasting; see the shaft of God. Lo! the death-shaft! It is whizzing in the air! it has pierced his heart! He falls! he falls! and with him Babel falls! That feast was a feast of death. 'Better to go to the house of mourning than to the house of feasting' such as that. I have read thy record, O mistress of the house! I say, woman! I have read thy record, and

> it is enough. I need not cross thy threshold; I do not want to see thy magnificent temple; I never wish to sit in thy splendid halls. It is enough! I am satisfied. Rather would I sleep nightly in my shroud, and sit on my coffin, and have my gravestone in the wall of my study, and live in a vault forever, than I would enter that house of feasting. Good God! may I be kept from sinful mirth! may I be kept from the house of sinful feasting! may I never be tempted to cross that threshold! O! then, young man, who art enchanted by its gayety, charmed by its music, stay! stay! for every plank in the floor is rotten, every stone that is there is dug from the quarries of hell; and if thou enterest into that house, thou shalt find that her steps lead down to hell, and go down to the chambers of everlasting woe."

It has often been remarked, that the sermons of Whitefield are destitute of striking remarks and gems of thought, and that they do not betray extensive reading, or afford much food for the understanding. A shrewd critic is of opinion that though Mr. Spurgeon's sermons do not display such broad flashes of eloquence, and such gifts and graces of declamation, yet their efficiency is of a higher and better grade, because they are addressed more to the twofold nature of man—the intelligence not less than the feelings. Accordingly, his sermons abound in sayings, allusions, and metaphors, which suggest thought and nourish meditation. Here are a few of them:

Although my house is not so with God.

> "It is necessary that you should have an 'although' in your lot, because if you had not, you know what you would do: you would build a very downy nest on the earth, and there you would lie down in sleep. It was said by the old writers that the nightingale never sang so sweetly as when she sat among thorns, since,

say they, the thorns prick her breast and remind her of her song. So God puts a thorn in your nest in order that you may sing. Your soul, without trouble, would be as a sea without tide or motion; it would become foul and noxious. As Coleridge describes the sea after a wondrous calm, so would the soul breed contagion and death."

Ambition in the churches.

"The next enemy to peace is ambition. 'Diotrephes loveth to have the preeminence,' and that fellow hath spoiled many a happy church. A man does not want, perhaps, to be preeminent, but then he is afraid that another should be, and so he would have him put down. Thus, brethren are finding fault; they are afraid that such a one will go too fast, and that such another will go too fast. The best way is to try to go as fast as he does. It is no use finding fault because some have a little preeminence. After all, what is the preeminence? It is the preeminence of one little animalcule over another. Look in a drop of water. One of these little fellows is five times as big as another, but we never think of that. I dare say he is very large, and thinks 'I have the preeminence inside my drop.' So we live in the little drop of the world, not much bigger in God's esteem than a drop of the bucket; and one of us seems a little larger than the other; a worm a little above his fellow-worms. But, O how big we get! and we want to get a little bigger, to get a little more prominent; but what is the use of it? for when we get ever so big, we shall then be so small that an angel would not find us out if God did not tell him where we were. Who ever heard up in heaven anything about emperors and kings, small, tiny insects? God can see the animalcule, therefore he can see us; but if he had not an eye to see the minutest, he would never discover us."

Memory.

"O! my friends, is it not too sadly true that we can recollect anything but Christ, and forget nothing so easily as him whom we ought to remember! While memory will preserve a poisonous weed, it suffereth the Rose of Sharon to wither."

Troubles are needful clogs to the soul.

"Some people call troubles weights. Verily they are so. But if trials be weights, I will tell you of a happy secret. There is such a thing as making a weight lift you. Give me pulleys and certain appliances, and I can make a weight lift me up. A gentleman once asked a friend concerning a beautiful horse of his, feeding about in the pasture with a clog on his foot, 'Why do you clog such a noble animal?' 'Sir,' he said, 'I would a great deal sooner clog him than lose him; he is given to leaping hedges.' That is why God clogs his people. They want a tether to prevent their straying, and then God binds them with afflictions to keep them near him."

The journey of life.

"What varied scenes the traveler will behold! Sometimes he will be on the mountains; anon he will descend into the valleys; here he will be where the brooks shine like silver, where the birds warble, where the air is balmy and the trees are green, and luscious fruits hang down to gratify his taste; anon he will find himself in the arid desert, where no life is found, and no sound is heard except the screech of the wild eagle in the air, where he finds no rest for the sole of his foot—the burning sky above him and the hot sand beneath him—no roof, no tree and no rock to shelter himself; at another time in a sweet oasis, resting himself by the springs of water, and plucking fruit from palm-trees. One moment he walks between the rocks in some narrow gorge where all is darkness; at another time he ascends the

> hill Mizar; now he descends into the valley of Baca; and he climbs the hill of Bashan, a high hill is the hill of Bashan; and yet again going into a den of leopards, he suffers trial and afflictions: such is life—ever changing."

Like Christmas Evans, our preacher occasionally makes use of allegory, and gives life, complexion, and action to some of the sermons by the employment of domestic personifications; but our space will not allow us to quote some beautiful passages of this description, which we had marked.

It is not possible by so few extracts to give any sufficient notion of Mr. Spurgeon's power as a preacher. And some of those who shall read all his sermons, from beginning to end, may be disappointed in not meeting with more of those nicer literary excellencies, which they have been accustomed to admire. Such should consider that as this young Timothy's mission is to move multitudes of the ignorant and thoughtless; it is the part of wisdom in him to paint in that bold fresco, which at once strikes all eyes and moves all hearts, rather than in that delicate miniature, which might please the glassed eye of the connoisseur, but which could not be so much as seen by a great crowd of the common people. It is this very kind of preaching, which is but folly to the philosopher, and but blundering to the critic, that, after all, somehow converts philosophers and brings even critics to repentance. Let the reader further consider that much, which renders any popular sermon effectual, is not to be printed. The melodies of the voice, the language of the eye, the graces of gesture, and the enlivening presence of a vast congregation cannot be reduced to writing. Once see and hear the man, and then you sit down and find meanings in his printed sermons, which mere words cannot express. A nobleman that went to see the sword with which Scanderberg had performed his great exploits, remarked, with a disappointed air, "The sword is no great matter, after all." "True," said a by-stander, "but your lordship will please recollect that you see only the sword, and not the arm that wielded it."

Mr. Spurgeon's style is simple, terse, easy, idiomatic and picturesque. It is remarkably free from mannerisms, being natural, and therefore lively, flexible and variable. At most times, he talks right on, in a plain, prudent, common sense way, and yet he has a peculiar command of good, old-fashioned English, while he is by no means deficient in the knowledge of its most modern elements, he always wisely prefers to employ the Saxon. His sentences are rather laconic than periodic, and as he does not think in long, connected trains of argumentation, the successive sentences are separate dictates of the intellect, such as the generality can readily comprehend. There is in many of them a self-sufficient, head-strong fling, and a firm, stalking tramp, which mark the peculiar movements of his mind. Still he has nothing of the measured tread and slow evolutions of Milton and Jeremy Taylor, nor has he the circumlocution of Chalmers, Edward Irving, and Henry Melville—those divines who declare the will of heaven while they are walking round in a circle. The gyromancies of these last would quite confound and bewilder many of Mr. Spurgeon's plain and unlearned auditors. His method is simple and lucid, but he never allows it to hamper his imagination or to curb his feelings. He often descends to the familiar and colloquial, than he ascends to the sublime and awful, for which he has a high, though not the highest, capacity.

With respect to his habits of composition, he assured us that not one word of his sermons is written before delivery, and that the only use he makes of his pen upon them is to correct the errors of the stenographer. His happy faculty of mere mental composition, and of remembering what he thus composes, saves him much time and drudgery. He can exercise it anywhere, but probably with more success in the pulpit, while he is giving utterance to what he has pre-arranged in his mind. Learning not to need manuscript out of the pulpit is the best preparation for not needing it in the pulpit; and he who, in his study, can think well independently of it, will, in the pulpit, think better without it; for the excitement occasioned by speaking what he has premeditated—if that excitement does not produce too deep feeling—will summon new thoughts to fill up the old ranks, and lead whole divisions of fresh recruits into the field.

It would be sacrilegious to subject to severe criticism sermons, which have been the channels of saving grace to so many sinners; have received the imprimatur of heaven, and have been so eagerly heard and so extensively read by great numbers of every class of society, and of all Christian denominations. Even the vipers of the London press, who have been accustomed to render unto God and unto Caesar nothing but black and unmingled venom, have forgotten their malice while listening to this young preacher, and witnessing, if not feeling, the blessed effects of the grace and truth of which he is the instrument. Nevertheless, we may speak of some of the faults of his preaching, if we do it without irreverence and without censoriousness. His sermons display an exuberance of fancy, and an inordinate love of poetic quotations, in the frequent introduction of which his good memory is by far too prompt and complaisant. These lines of poetry are often so woven into the prose as to pass for original matter with those who are not deeply read in the effusions of the muses, and more than one critic—and we are perhaps among the number—has admired as his own what he had borrowed, and carelessly thrown among his own. Then there are many fine little phrases and sentences of his, which display more fancy than is compatible with the force and fervor of natural composition. Let him give us more imagination and less fancy the wild flowers of an uncultivated soil are always attractive where they are not too numerous. Corinna, the learned Theban lady, reproved Pindar, whom she had five times overcome in a trial of skill, for having scattered the flowers of Parnassus too prodigally through all his works, remarking to him that men sow with the hand, and not with the sack. However, we may reasonably hope that the lapse of years and the maturity of the faculties will substitute ripe fruit for these natural blessings of youth.

There is another fault still more boyish, but showing a far less certain sign of promise. We refer to the dismal punning in which he has more than once indulged. In his sermon, "Storming of the Battlements," he thus sorrily amuses himself:—

> "Says the man, 'I can make myself better.'—O, blessed day when God directs his shot against that. I know I hugged that old idea a long while, with my 'cans,' 'cans,' 'cans;' but I found my 'cans' would hold no water, and suffered all I put in to run out." Hear another: "Ah! ye who have never been entranced by the precious sound contained in that word, Jesu; ye who know not that Jesu means I-ES-U ('I ease you'), ye have lost the joy and comfort of your lives, and must live miserable and unhappy."

We need not say that so heinous a pun is a great blot upon a sermon. It is hardly deserving of a place among the quibbles of the Rabbins, the interpretations of the Cabalists, or the Rosicrucians.

Mr. Spurgeon is wont to exercise a censorship over his brethren in the ministry, which seems rather to offend than to improve them. Like some of our own evangelists, he helps to swell the ribald outcry of the profane against the ministry in general. Now, instead of holding up to public scorn, solitary cases of clerical folly and dullness, impiety and unfaithfulness, and then by sweeping assertions, spreading that scorn over the entire ministry of England, and by implication telling his audiences that it is the fault of their pastors that they did not repent long ago—ought he not rather to show them that their condemnation is all the heavier because they have not heeded the minister whom they have been permitted to hear. "Pride, covetousness and envy," says Luther, "are three dogs that should never be allowed to come into the pulpit." Mr. Spurgeon is not covetous, and he has no occasion to envy either the gifts or the graces of any preacher now living. It can only be pride that can prompt him to look down with contempt upon those whose talents and acquirements mate them able and successful preachers and pastors for the few rather than for the many. Who was the instrument of Mr. Spurgeon's own conversion? A man of his own talents—a man capable of causing such a general excitement and furor? Far from it. He was, according to his own account of him, "a tall, thin man, with a feeble voice," who preached "in a little place of worship." A man whom he had never seen from that day, and probably never will see until they meet in heaven. May not Mr. Spurgeon, without any neglect of his prophetic vocation, be a little more charitable to those ministers whom neither nature nor grace has qualified to follow in his own steps? There are, no doubt, in London, many pastors under whose care not a few of the young converts in the New Park-street church might place themselves, with a better hope than they now have a right to entertain, of growing up to be men and women in faith, in knowledge and in charity. Shall this Paul who plants, tax with inefficiency Apollos who waters, because he cannot plant also? Why may not men of different gifts discover in each other the same spirit, and their equal relation to the work of contributing to the perfection of the saints? Why should not the son of thunder give the right hand of fellowship to the son of consolation? Why should not the evangelist cordially cooperate with the pastor, and the pastor with the evangelist, and all with the missionary?

Our young preacher has also added to the number of his adversaries by denouncing the whole system of collegiate and theological education now in operation throughout the world. He recommends that those who are called to the ministry be placed under the tuition of some pastor for the acquisition of all the knowledge and wisdom requisite for their work. We will not here dilate on a question, which is already practically, and as we think, wisely, settled, at least in our land, and for the present generation of American pastors.

The question has often been asked on both sides of the Atlantic—"What is the great secret of Mr. Spurgeon's popularity?" It has seemed to us that all those who have publicly ventured an opinion on this point, have failed because they have hazarded a generalization from one or two darling facts. We rather incline to the view that we should take into the account not only all Mr. Spurgeon's peculiar talents and attractions, but especially also the grace and providence of God. This is, if we mistake not, his own way of regarding his success. He confesses that he sees a thousand chances, as men would call them, all working together like wheels in a great machine, to fix him just where he is; and he looks back to a hundred places where if one of those little wheels had run awry, he might have been occupying a very different position.

We must confess that for ourselves, the spectacle, which is presented by Mr. Spurgeon's preaching to the poor of London, is more affecting than the hearing of the most pathetic strains of his eloquence.

No wonder that it cheered the sad heart of John the Baptist, when in prison he was told that Christ was preaching glad tidings to the poor, and that it prepared him joyfully to lay down his neck for his fidelity to the souls of the rich. See what crowds of artisans are turning away from the halls of the political meetings, of the infidel lectures, and the minor theaters, to gather about Mr. Spurgeon's pulpit. See the weary laborers of Bankside going to hear him even on the nights of the week days. See 12,000 of the working people of Bethnal Green, flocking around him in the open field at Hackney. Take a nearer view. Fix your eyes on individuals here and there. See the poor harlot, who was a few minutes ago passing the doors of the New Park-street chapel, determined to cast herself off Blackfriars Bridge. She thought she would step in and for the last time hear something that will prepare her to stand before her Maker. She is just in time to hear the text, "Seest thou this woman?" The preacher speaks of Mary Magdalen, her sins, her washing the Saviour's feet with her tears, and wiping them with the hair of her head. There stands the woman, melted with the thoughts of her own past life, as she hears it described, and more melted with the description of the pardoning love of Jesus. Thus is she saved from death, temporal and eternal. Go and hear him, ye Thackerays, who satirize the lying, the lust, and the vanity of the English aristocracy, without offering any remedy therefore. There is a man who is offering the remedy to the vices of some even of these. Go and hear him, ye Dickenses, whose stories of the shame, the loneliness, the misery, and the patience of London's poor, have dissolved many a fine lady in tears, without opening her hand to imploring woe. There is a man of liberal and loving soul, who actually shakes hands with all this dirt and rags, searches for the hearts that are buried beneath it, and holds them up to the light of the cross, where they fledge their wings and soar to the glories of heaven. Go and hear him, ye who are secretly glorying in the large donations ye have made for the benefit of the poor. There you will find a man who in body, soul, spirit, and grace, is God's own donation to the poor, preaching to them the good old gospel of his grace, in good old English words, and, by the aid of his good Spirit, leading them to the Good Shepherd, "God's unspeakable gift."

OUTLINE OF MR. SPURGEON'S CREED

Many strange rumors having been put into circulation respecting the doctrines preached by Mr. Spurgeon, before he had been in London a year, it was thought desirable to publish a new edition of that most estimable summary of doctrine, the *Baptist Confession of Faith*, as drawn up and signed by thirty-seven Baptist ministers in the year 1689. This edition, revised by Mr. Spurgeon, who added to it a preface, was published in the autumn of 1855. The articles are thirty-two in number, of which the following is an outline, little more than the names of the successive articles being here given, the reader being referred to the work itself for further details.

I. That the *Holy Scripture* is the only sufficient rule of faith.

II. That God is *one*, consisting of *three* subsistences—the Father, the Word and Holy Spirit.

III. That God hath *decreed all things*. That some men and angels are predestinated to eternal life; and others being left to act in their sin to their just condemnation.

IV. That God the Father, Son, and Holy Ghost, did *create* the world in six days.

V. That God, in his *providence*, doth uphold, direct, dispose, and govern all creatures and things.

VI. That man was created upright; that by sin, he *fell* from original righteousness, and his sin is imputed to all mankind.

VII. That God made a *covenant of grace*, offering life and salvation by that covenant through Jesus Christ.

VIII. That the Lord Jesus is ordained the *Mediator* between God and man.

IX. That God hath indued the *will of man* with natural liberty, and power of acting upon choice: that is, *free-will.*

X. That those whom God hath predestinated unto life, he is pleased in his own time *effectually to call* by his Word and Spirit, out of a state of sin and death, to grace and salvation. Infants that die in infancy are saved by Christ, through the Spirit.

XI. Those whom God calleth, he *justifieth*, by pardoning their sins, and accepting them as righteous.

XII. That all those that are justified, God makes them partakers of the grace of *adoption.*

XIII. That those who are called, and regenerate, through the death of Christ, are also *sanctified.*

XIV. That the *faith* whereby the elect are enabled to believe for *salvation* is the work of the Spirit of Christ.

XV. That such of the elect as live in sin for many years, God in their effectual calling, giveth them *repentance unto life and salvation.*

XVI. That *good works* are only such as God hath commanded, such as are the fruits of a lively faith; that our best works cannot merit the pardon of sin.

XVII. That those whom God hath called, and sanctified, can neither totally nor finally fall from grace, but shall *persevere therein to the end.*

XVIII. That such as truly believe in the Lord Jesus, may in this life be certainly *assured* that they are in a state of grace and salvation.

XIX. That God gave to Adam a *law of obedience*; that the *moral law* given on Sinai doth forever bind all, as well justified persons as others to obedience thereof.

XX. That the covenant of works being broken by sin, God was pleased to give the promise of Christ and salvation by him, which is revealed only in the Word of God. That Christ is revealed in the Gospel, which revelation is *sufficient to the saving of all men.*

XXI. That *Christian liberty* consists in freedom from the guilt of sin, and from the yoke and curse of the law. That God hath left the conscience free from the doctrines and commandments of men.

XXII. That God is to be *worshiped*; that *religious worship* is to be given to God the Father, the Son, and the Holy Spirit, and to him alone. That religious worship is required of all; and that the *Sabbath be kept holy* unto the Lord.

XXIII. That a *lawful oath* is a part of religious worship, and should be taken with holy fear and reverence; that vows be made to God alone, and performed sacredly.

XXIV. That the *civil magistrate* is set over the people to promote the glory of God and the public good, by maintaining justice and peace. That we should pray for kings and all that are in authority.

XXV. That *marriage* is to be between one man and one woman; that all people with sound judgment may marry, but within the degrees of affinity.

XXVI. That *the church* consists of the whole number of the elect throughout the world professing the faith of the gospel, and obedience unto God by Christ; the Lord Jesus Christ is the head of the church; that the Pope of Rome is anti-Christ; that church members are saints by calling; that pastors and other gifted persons may preach; that believers are bound to join particular churches. Provision is also made for offenses, difficulties and differences.

XXVII. That all saints united to Jesus Christ should have *fellowship with him* and with each other.

XXVIII. That *baptism* and the *Lord's Supper* are positive ordinances to be continued to the end of time.

XXIX. That *baptism* is an ordinance of the New Testament, a sign of the believer's fellowship with Christ; that those only are proper subjects for baptism who profess repentance toward God and faith in our Lord Jesus Christ; that immersion or dipping in water is necessary to the due administration of this ordinance.

XXX. That the *Supper of the Lord* is to be observed to the end of the world, as a remembrance of the sacrifice and death of Christ, and for the confirmation and spiritual nourishment of believers. That ignorant and ungodly persons may not partake of those holy mysteries.

XXXI. That the bodies of men after death return to dust, and their souls have an immortal subsistence; the righteous are admitted into heaven, the wicked are cast into hell. That all the *dead shall be raised* up with the self-same bodies at the last day, and shall be united to their souls forever.

XXXII. That at the *last judgment*, all the world shall be judged by Jesus Christ. That the Day of Judgment shall be unknown to men until it shall arrive, that all may be constantly prepared for the coming of the Lord.

APPENDIX

After so much has been said in the body of this work of the estimation in which Mr. Spurgeon's sermons are held by those who give tone to public sentiment in the religious and literary world, it may appear superfluous to make further extracts from the numberless commentary notices of the press. Yet it is due to a man who has been most wantonly and unjustly assailed, not only by criticism, but also by the grossest and most exaggerated misrepresentations, to present, in a condensed and comprehensive form, the testimonies of intelligent and impartial men.

FROM *THE NEW YORK OBSERVER*
Sermons by the Rev. C.H. Spurgeon.
New York: Sheldon, Blakeman & Co.

"A second series by the young preacher whose fame is so widespread, and whose popularity in London is so great that no house can be obtained adequate to the crowds, which hang upon his ministry. We have been reading the discourses to discover if in them lies the charm that attracts the multitude. We find them, as far as we have read, to be evangelical, in doctrine strongly Calvinistic, eminently Scriptural in illustration and proof, and intensely glowing with the terrors of the law, which he presents with boldness, severity and power. We scarcely ever meet with a word or phrase that is coarse, no attempt to excite a smile, but we find a solemnity of thought, and a weight of feeling that speak a soul deeply in earnest, and seeking the salvation of others. We do rejoice that the crowds who flock to hear must listen to such preaching as this. It is adapted to make a deep impression on the sinner, and we should consider the preacher to be a prayerful man, feeling his dependence on divine aid, and looking to God to give the Holy Spirit to make the word effectual. After having said so much, it is not worthwhile to add criticism.

"The preacher is a mere boy, twenty-two years of age, and if he has been puffed up with praise, and made somewhat egotistical, it is no wonder. We confess our surprise that he knows so much, and can speak with such fervid eloquence, and sustains such efforts as he makes; and however he may be criticized, we cannot but regard him as the most remarkable young preacher of the age. This volume will add to his reputation in this country."

FROM THE *NEW YORK EVANGELIST*

There is no gift of Christ to his church for which she has more reason devoutly to thank her Lord and Head, than that of a man to preach the gospel. Not a mere automaton; a repeater of other men's thoughts, and a dissembler of their emotions; a glib reciter of formal creeds, or a mumbler of prescribed formulas of devotion; producing an impression of extraordinary sanctity by solemn grimace and whining tones, but a true, living man—one who has thought for himself, and learned by hard experience; who, out of the struggles of his own mind with doubt and despair, has at length come to believe; and who, in the bitterness of remorse, has found peace and forgiveness by penitence and prayer; and who thus is able to speak to other men from the fresh thoughts of his own mind, and the deep experience of his own tried, tempted and suffering soul. Such a man—clear in thought and strong in faith, of bold spirit and eloquent voice—alone seems worthy to be the herald of religion, and fitted to assert its just supremacy in human affairs.

Such preachers are not very common in our day. Yet we have had on both sides of the Atlantic some kingly examples—here, Mason and Griffin, and there, Chalmers and Robert Hall and Edward Irving. The latter of these was long our special study and admiration. It is many years since we read his *Orations for the Oracles of God*, and his *Argument for Judgment* to come, as he called his fiery discourses, dropping the very name of *Sermon*, as of itself sufficient to inspire drowsiness and slumber. At that time, he seemed to us the very type of manhood in the preacher—one of the old prophets come again—a John the Baptist preaching repentance to a sinful and adulterous generation. Here, says Carlyle, "was a man who strove to be a priest in an age alien to the character." This erratic genius was caught and lionized in London, as a wild Cameronian, fresh from the Grampian Hills, and men crowded to hear his impetuous eloquence. The excitement of great popularity and immense labor did its work upon his body and brain, but it took the modern Babylon, with its roar and strife, its loud applause and bitter censures, ten years to kill him.

Such was the impression made by his extraordinary career, that when we visited London, almost the first spot to which we made a pilgrimage was the chapel in which he preached. As we stood in his pulpit, we saw again the mighty audiences to which he once thundered, crowded with the rank and wealth and wit of England; with Brougham and Canning and Sir James Mackintosh hanging upon his lips; orators and generals and statesmen, all bowing before the eloquence of the preacher—like English oaks rocking in the storm. At that moment, we noticed that the pulpit was draped in black, and asking the cause, were told it was for Dr. Chalmers. It was the first we had heard of his death. Thus at the same moment, we were reminded of the loss of the two great preachers of Scotland—perhaps the most effective pulpit orators of modern times.

It is sad to think of such giants passing away, and we fear that their place can never be filled. Mournfully, we repeat,

"We ne'er shall look upon their like again."

But when kings die, princes succeed to their thrones, who sometimes are found not unworthy to bear their fathers' sceptres. So it may be that God will raise up other men in London and Edinburg, in England and America, to preach with the same power and success. Within a year or two, our readers may have seen frequent notices of a young preacher who has appeared in London and attracted great attention, causing a sensation hardly equaled since the days of Edward Irving. From the first, we have been suspicious of this new prodigy. Some passages, quoted from his sermons, seemed so full of egotism and so wanting in taste, that we set him down as a mountebank in the pulpit; a compound of small talents with inordinate vanity; with just enough of dramatic skill to make a London audience gape and stare, while the staple of his discourse was made up of low illustrations and threadbare anecdotes. We judged him, therefore, to be master of a little stage effect, but wholly destitute of anything that might be considered as remarkable for either intellect or eloquence.

But a second volume of his sermons has lately appeared from the press of Messrs. Sheldon, Blakeman & Co., to which we have given more attention, and in which we are obliged to confess the unmistakable signs of power. In these, we see few traces of that rhetorical claptrap by which charlatans contrive to attract attention. There is little of that high-flown rhetoric, which makes the vulgar gape, and which sometimes passes for eloquence. Indeed, the style is remarkable for simplicity. The sentences are short, and the words are chiefly of the old, vigorous Saxon. The plain, homely phrases often remind us of the pat and pithy expressions of John Bunyan, whom Spurgeon has evidently studied much, and seems to have taken as a model of style. While he often treats of the doctrines of the Bible, he introduces no metaphysical distinctions, no theological refinements; he never reasons abstractly, but by analogy, by illustration, and by example. Thus, all is made plain to the humblest comprehension.

His sermons abound in illustrations, which are always simple, and yet often very felicitous and beautiful. He is also full of anecdotes, and tells a story with great effect. The impression of these is heightened by his remarkable, dramatic talent, in which he resembles Gough, or Father Taylor, the sailor's preacher of Boston. Mingled with these vivid pictures are frequent quotations of spirit-stirring hymns, which quicken the blood like the sound of a trumpet. When to these elements of power, we add a voice of such compass as to be heard distinctly by an assembly of 10,000 persons, we are at no loss to understand his great popularity. But his object is not merely entertainment. Overriding all is an earnest purpose to do good. Under these similes and illustrations is the plain gospel truth, earnestly applied to the hearts and consciences of men. His sermons abound in direct appeals to the hearers. The preacher speaks, not to mankind in general, but to those right before him, to the tradesmen and working-people of London. As we read these fervid discourses, we can easily imagine their effect upon such an audience. None can doubt that the crowds that flock to hear this eloquent young preacher go away pricked in conscience, humbled in heart,

> and often reformed in life. With this altered impression of the man, we rejoice in the raising up of such an earnest and faithful preacher of Christ, in the heart of England, and we are inclined to predict great good from his labors. It is too soon to say that he will be another Chalmers or Robert Hall. He is yet in the morning of his career. He began to preach very young, and is still but twenty-three years old. Some are ready to "despise his youth," as if such a boy could not know anything, or say anything worthy of listening. But what if he be young? So was Summerfield. Larned, of New Orleans, died when he was but twenty-four, and yet he was, at that moment, perhaps the most eloquent preacher in America. Thomas Spencer, of Liverpool, closed his career at twenty, but he had already thrilled tens of thousands by his eloquence. Youth indeed is liable to great mistakes from ignorance and inexperience; but it has also great advantages in its robust vitality and natural fervor and enthusiasm.
>
> There is indeed danger that a young man, lifted into sudden popularity, may be puffed up with conceit, and so be given up to suffer a humiliating fall. This young pulpit celebrity is certainly exposed to great danger. His best friends must pray that he be not spoiled by flattery. But if this be avoided, and his life and health be spared—if the remorseless London public do not kill him, as they killed Edward Irving—he may prove a great blessing to the church and to England.

The following was contributed to the columns of the *New York Observer* by a distinguished pastor of a Presbyterian church in New York, whose fame as a preacher and teacher of theology is world-wide:

> "The religious public is much divided about Mr. Spurgeon, some saying, 'He is a good man,' and others, 'Nay, but he deceiveth

the people;' some extolling him as a new wonder of evangelical eloquence, and others stigmatizing him as a ranter, a charlatan and a pulpit merry-andrew. We avow ourselves to be among the number of those who bless God that our day has witnessed the rise of one so well fitted to startle and electrify the indolent and godless masses of the great modern Babylon into religious interest; and we wish there were today a hundred such as he in London, and fifty such in New York. While we, more nice and dainty preachers, come weekly before our well-dressed and decorous assemblies with sermons compounded according to all the rules, and read with every observance of orthoëpy, there are a hundred thousand poor people without, who do not come near us, and who would perhaps go to sleep if they did. If God intends the 'common people' to be roused into a great religious revolution, and the rapidly degenerating populace of London and New York to be awakened, he will raise up Whitefields, Rowland Hills and Spurgeons. Just so preached Luther and Latimer; the likenesses extending even to the odd and sometimes ludicrous expressions, which are not indeed to our taste, but which abound even more in the reported sermons of Whitefield, and which belong to the idiosyncrasy of the men. A greater fault is the frequent putting forward of his own personality; but all of these are specks upon a fair and brilliant disk.

"*Mr. Spurgeon preaches the truth of God*; let this be always borne in mind; and he preaches it to 10,000 at a time. Is not this a fact to be rejoiced? We do not mean his tenet concerning baptism, nor his tenet concerning the Second Advent, neither of which is made prominent; we will not underwrite any of his crotchets of opinion, or his particular expositions of Scripture; but we recognize in his constant teachings the great evangelical and saving doctrines of the New Testament and the Westminster

Assembly. Mr. Spurgeon shows in every sermon that he has been a diligent reader, not only of the Bible, but also of theology. To this, he owes much of his force. The family terms of old Non-conformist divinity fall freely from his lips, and he affectionately names their great authors. The outcry against him is sufficiently accounted for by his brandishing the terrors of the law, by his exalting the free grace of the gospel, and by his constant and unflinching avowal of Calvinism. Nothing that has yet been uttered against him in the way of vituperation equals the assaults upon Mr. Whitefield, both in England and America. No one needs to be informed how much is lost when we read the cold-written reports of imaginative and impassioned eloquence. The sermons of Dean Kirwan and of Whitefield are striking instances. Yet no one can peruse a single sermon of Mr. Spurgeon's without feeling himself to be within the grasp of a great, undisciplined, and daring genius, who, amid some foibles and numberless violations of taste, wields the sword of a champion, and is all on fire with zeal for God. We heartily agree with our honored friend, Dr. Wayland, that the world and the church need such preachers; and looking downhill toward the close of our own work, with many regrets over wrong methods, we rejoice and hope at the sight of young men brought into the field with such energies and success. Even where the standard of homiletics is not ours, 'Christ is preached, and we therein do rejoice, yea, and will rejoice.'"

FROM *HARPER'S WEEKLY*

Sermons of the Rev. C.H. Spurgeon, of London. Second Series. New York: Sheldon, Blakeman & Co.

The portrait, which is given in this book of the young preacher who draws such immense houses in London, represents him as a full-faced, fat, boyish-looking man, of twenty-two or twenty-three years old, and it is doubtless a correct likeness. Young as he is, his sermons are tremendous in their effect. Their faults are prominent and great—the faults of extreme youth and inexperience both in the world and in rhetoric—but their virtues are also very great. He is in the main what would be called an orthodox Calvinist in sentiment, while his style of preaching is directed to the consciences and hearts of his hearers. We can readily imagine the effect which some of these bold, daring appeals must have on the minds of hearers when hurled at them from the sacred desk. Much there is in Mr. Spurgeon's eloquence that is admirable; much that is thrilling, overpowering; but, at the same time, there is much that is startling. With the abstract doctrine contained in his sermon on election, we suppose no Calvinist of the straitest sect would find fault; but the manner of the concluding appeal strikes us as the coolest piece of argument that has of yet been addressed by a clergyman to a sinner. This is an extract from it:

"O sinner, come to the throne of electing mercy. Thou mayest die where thou art. Go to God; and, even supposing he should spurn thee, suppose his uplifted hand should drive thee away—a thing impossible—yet thou wilt not lose anything; thou wilt not be the more damned for that. Besides, supposing thou be damned, thou wouldst have the satisfaction at least of being able to lift up thine eyes in hell and say, 'God, I asked mercy of thee, and thou wouldst not grant it; I sought it, but thou didst refuse it.'"

The peculiarity of Mr. Spurgeon's style is in his brief, strong sentences. His words are short, sharp and telling. He never goes around a truth; never wraps it up to administer it; never attempts to touch his cannon off softly. If he lives twenty years, he will repent of his present sins and be a greater preacher. For the present, this book is the most readable collection of sermons, without exception, that has ever found its way to our hands, and will repay the purchaser a hundred-fold.

CORRESPONDENCE OF *THE NEW YORK INDEPENDENT*

Great orators, whether pulpit, platform, or senatorial, make many friends and many foes. This being inevitable, we are at no loss to account for the applause and contumely, which have been profusely heaped upon the young minister, the Rev. C.H. Spurgeon, whose appearance and labors in the metropolis have excited in all religious circles, and even beyond them, attention and surprise, and in some instances unbounded admiration. Scarcely more than a youth in years, comparatively untutored, and without a name, he enters the greatest city in the world, and almost simultaneously commands audiences larger than have usually listened to her most favored preachers. Almost daily has he occupied pulpits in various parts of town and country, and everywhere been greeted by overflowing congregations.

As might be expected, many who have listened to him have gone away to speak ill of his name; while others, and by far the greater number, have been instructed by his arguments, melted by his appeals, and stimulated by his earnestness. There have been seen among his hearers ministers of mark, of nearly every section of the Christian church; laymen well known in all circles as the supporters of the benevolent and evangelical institutions of the day; citizens of renown, from the chief magistrate down to the parish beadle; and Holyoake, the editor of the infidel serial, *The Reasoner*, has, by his own confession, been among his hearers. That the man who causes such a furor must possess some power not commonly found in men of his profession, will only be doubted by his prejudiced detractors. Whether that power be physical, intellectual, or moral, or a happy blending of them all, is, perhaps, a question not yet ripe for decision.

It cannot be disputed that Mr. Spurgeon is in various respects an extraordinary man. Never, since the days of George Whitefield and Edward Irving, has any minister of religion acquired so great a reputation as this Baptist preacher in so short a time. Here is a mere youth—a perfect stripling, only twenty-one years of age—incomparably the most popular preacher of the day. There is no man in Great Britain who could draw such immense audiences; and none who, in his happiest efforts, can so completely enthrall the attention and delight the minds of his hearers. While the enlargement of his chapel in New Park-street was taking place, Mr. Spurgeon preached in Exeter Hall; but this spacious building soon proved far too small to hold the crowds who thronged to hear the youthful Boanerges. It was no unusual sight on a Sunday evening to see placards put up outside the building announcing that the Hall was full, and that no more could be admitted. Since the enlargement of his chapel, which is now capable of holding 1,800 people, it has been found necessary for the police to be present at every service, and the pew-holders are admitted by ticket through a side door. This accomplished, at ten minutes prior to the commencement of the service, the front doors are opened and a rush commences; but it is speedily over, for the chapel is full—not only the seats, but also every inch of standing-room being occupied, and the gates have to be closed, with an immense crowd of disappointed expectant hearers outside.

Although some of Mr. Spurgeon's vilifiers speak of irreverence and witticisms, your correspondent, when he listened to the youthful evangelist, was especially impressed with the stillness and solemnity pervading the entire service. Some of his appeals to the conscience, some of his remonstrances with the careless, constituted specimens of a very high order of oratorical power. When pronouncing the doom of those who live and die in a state of impenitence, he makes hundreds of his congregation quail and quake in their seats. He places their awful destiny in such vivid colors before their eyes that they almost imagine they are already in the regions of darkness and despair. In his preface to a volume of sermons just published, he tells us that such has been the impression produced by some of his sermons that he has ascertained upward of twenty cases of conversion as the result of one discourse, to say nothing of those instances of a saving change wrought on his hearers, which will be unknown until the world to come has made its important and unexpected revelations.

When this able and eloquent preacher first made his appearance in the horizon of the religious world, and dazzled the masses in London by his brilliancy, many feared that he either might get intoxicated by the large draughts of popularity, which he had daily to drink, or that he would not be able, owing to the want of variety, to sustain the reputation he had so suddenly acquired. Neither result has happened. Whatever may be his defect, either as a man or as a preacher of the gospel, it is due to him to state that he has not been spoiled by popular applause. Constitutionally, he has no small amount of self-esteem; but so far from its growing with his daily extending fame, he appears to be more humble and more subdued than when he first burst on our astonished gaze. And with regard to the fear that his excellence as a preacher would not be sustained, the event has proved the groundlessness of such an apprehension. There is no falling off whatever. On the contrary, he is in not a few respects improving with the lapse of time. His striking originality can be seen to greater advantage than at first. There is no sameness in his sermons. The variety of his matter, not of course as regards his doctrines, but as relates to his expositions, illustrations and applications of divine truth, is as great as ever.

Mr. Spurgeon has been thought by many to entertain and advance the crude views of the hyper-Calvinists. He may, at times, lay himself open to such a charge; but, we verily believe, he has, in truth, little sympathy with those of the class referred to: his offer of a free gospel, and appeals to the sinner being sufficient evidence in the matter with all who know anything of the preachers of the Dr. Crisp school. It cannot be doubted that he holds Calvinistic views of Christianity, and proclaims this doctrine strongly and boldly, thus presenting himself and his preaching as a conspicuous mark for controversial censure. But there is a courageous and transparent consistency characterizing the man and his mission that ought most assuredly to neutralize all unfair and bitter criticism.

It must be evident to all who have read Mr. Spurgeon's sermons that he is no superficial thinker. He has long been a diligent and earnest seeker after truth, and is theoretically and experimentally acquainted with much of the deep spirituality of divine truth. He must have studied profoundly Leighton's writings and Wesley's hymns; for he has much of the experience of Wesley, and a high degree of the spirituality of Leighton. Some have said that William Jay, of Bath, and Robert Hall, of Bristol, are the models on which he has sought to mold his style of address; but he needs the logical acumen of the one, and the polished elegance of diction, which characterized the other. He has, however, their better qualities of thorough devotion to the service of the gospel, and a power and pathos far transcending theirs. But he is too originally constituted to be an imitator, and is more likely to found a style of his own, than to imitate that of another. True, he has much of Rowland Hill's quaintness of illustration, and not infrequently provokes a smile by some startling expression or figure; but the general seriousness and earnestness of his tone and manner forbid any feeling of levity; and if occasionally his humor excites a passing smile, the depth of his pathos more frequently draws tears from the greater part of his congregation.

During the year 1855, Mr. Spurgeon's Sunday morning sermon has been regularly published in the course of the succeeding week for one penny, or two cents, and some of them have reached as high a sale as 60,000 copies. These fifty-three sermons are now republished in a neat volume, with a preface by Mr. Spurgeon, in which he states that he has documentary evidence that every sermon has received the seal of God's blessing, in having been employed as an instrument in the conversion of sinners to Christ. The volume is certain to have an immense sale; and from its circulation in every corner of the world where the English language is read, there is every reason to hope and believe that it will be productive of great good.

The London ministers generally have looked upon Mr. Spurgeon with coolness, and in some instances with dislike. Some noble exceptions there have been, such as the Rev. James Sherman, of Blackheath, and Dr. A. Fletcher, of Finsbury chapel. And even the Baptist Missionary Society so far yielded to the popular feeling in favor of Mr. Spurgeon, as to solicit him to preach one of the anniversary sermons for their Society this year. The religious press, too, has fearlessly stood by Mr. Spurgeon against his calumniators. *The London Patriot*, *Banner*, and *Christian News*, have commended this second Whitefield. May the Head of the church continue to hold this youthful Timothy as a star in his right hand, and through his instrumentality bring many souls to bow to the sceptre of his love!

Beta.

England, March 14, 1866

FROM *THE CHICAGO JOURNAL*

There used to be such a thing as "a call" to preach. Men that heard it obeyed, and "left their nets." Now, sometimes at least, they go without hearing, and to get nets—with fish in them.

A "call" is supposed to imply three things: disposition, ability and opportunity; that is, a door must be opened, and somebody waiting, who is able and willing to go in at it. What work those people make—and they are not few—who have two-thirds of a call to preach, needs no description at our hand.

To know how to *tell* what we know, is the rarest knowledge in the world, and yet, it is to truth, precisely what the range is to the powder—just the only thing that can render it effective.

We have heard men preach who were very much in the predicament of soldiers that blow up their own magazines without so much as singeing an enemy's eyebrow; magnificent fireworks, but no grape.

Of all intellectual cutlery, a sermon should be the keenest. It should not tear and mutilate; we have no fancy for a real war sword, and are not afraid of a hoe, but if the choice were left us with which implement our quietus should be made, we should give a verdict for the sword without leaving the court. In fact, a sermon should have the sort of edge and sweep to it that is supposed to belong to that good "Toledo" whose victims did not know they were being decapitated until their heads were gone entirely, whereupon they were in a worse condition than Briareus—but one pair of hands, and no head at all.

The beast of Balaam waited for the touch of the miraculous hand before he attempted to say anything, but this age of ours is faster than they were in Balaam's time, and the day of miracles has passed.

The world generally, we believe, is disposed to look leniently upon the sermon as a literary production, provided the author be honest and earnest and loving; if the world were less forgiving, we might have fewer sermons, but there would be a great deal more of them. To take a theme from the sacred page, as familiar to the mass of men in civilized communities as the household word "home," and so present it as to arrest the attention and interest the heart, is about as difficult as the capture of Gibraltar, and yet a thing attempted every week by multitudes of men, who begin to talk themselves into thought, and end by talking their theme into nothing, and their hearers into a drowse.

If one theme more than another deserves the choicest of illustration, the most sinewy of argument, and the most persuasive of appeal, that theme is Heaven and the hopes that hang on it, like dews upon the morning.

There seems to us, even at this far remove of the editorial chair, no office so grand as that he fills who stands, in the old but unworn stereotype of Sabbath phrase, "between two worlds," wherein, in the words of Napier, dwell those we love, and those we have loved; nothing so beautiful as the robing of a truth that contains no element of human frailty; but unsullied by the breath of passion, unsoiled by the fingers of mortality, is held aloft to the gaze of the great congregation, pure as the Southern Cross that bends in holy sign over the humblest sailor upon the sea.

How beautiful we have thought—ay, how beautiful we have seen—such a life may be, flying like a white dove with music in its wing, 'twixt earth and heaven. The time has gone by when we fancied "the minister" could never die; that even the lightning would respect his person, and flicker harmless around his head; that sweet faith of childhood has fled, for we have seen him laid to rest, and remembered, as they left him, how "He giveth his beloved sleep."

Nature found out the secret of his grave long ago, and claimed his dust for the uses of the budding spring, but the blamelessness of his life, the warmth of his heart, and the singleness of his purpose, composed the sublimest of sermons. No error of the uttered word, no faltering of the feeble voice, no lack of arrangement there, and so, though dead, he speaketh yet.

The style of men who were more eloquent in their works than they were in their words, is an old style, and fashions are changeful as the moon; the men who never forget their mission, nor put off their calling with their Sabbath-day attire, are becoming fewer, and we are constrained to believe that those who remain rather belong to a past age than to the present.

Truth walks a good deal, now-a-days, upon carpets in listed slippers; trenchant blades are wielded, but they are safe-housed in the scabbards. Nobody is harmed a hair, and over and over, is Sancho Panza's beatitude repeated: "Blessed is the man who invented sleep"; and there are numbers to claim it, and of course numbers to be blest; and so, blessed be poppies!
But besides these makers of the Sunday siesta, there are those who are not content to stand with the great Apostle to the Gentiles, upon Mars Hill, but they needs take up their abode on Sinai, and their tables of the law are all stone, and clouds and darkness are their chief delight.

Abou Ben Adhem is a heathenish name, but we wish every pulpit in the land had a Ben Adhem in it. "May his tribe increase!" Abou Ben Adhem, who

"Awoke, one night, from a deep dream of peace,
And saw, within the moonlight of his room,
Making it rich, and like a lily in bloom,
An angel writing in a book of gold.
Exceeding peace had made Ben Adhem bola,
And to the presence in the room he said:
'What writest thou?' The vision raised its head.
And, with a look made all sweet accord,
Answered—'The name of those who love the Lord.'
'And is mine one?' said Abou. 'Nay, not so,'
Replied the angel. Abou spoke more low,
But cheerily still, and said—'I pray thee then,
Write me as one that loves his fellow-men.'
The angel wrote, and vanished. The next night
It came again with a great wakening light,
And showed the names of those whom love of God had blessed,
And, lo! Ben Art hem's name led all the rest!"

Precious little as we know about preaching, such were the thoughts that we have been betrayed into expressing by the sermons of the Rev. C. H. Spurgeon of London.

SECOND SERIES.

Of this young man, who, like an unannounced comet, scintillated into the clerical sphere, the majority of our readers know something. Fervid in style, vivid in illustration, earnest in appeal, versed in biblical lore, his youth increased the wonder, he was at once rechristened a "Whitefield," and multitudes thronged to listen and applaud; and thus was inaugurated what, for want of a better term, we may call " a star engagement" in winning souls. We do not like the display that attends his ministrations; we do not see why the language should be beggared of its best adjectives to do him homage. If God has given him more talents than his neighbor, and he is employing them for God and the truth's sake, he is entitled to be numbered with that old man whose whole life was a sermon, and the place of whose grave is quite forgotten.

Mr. Spurgeon is an orator of wonderful power, as he must be whose syllables rise articulate above the Babel of London. We have here twenty-seven discourses, differing in thought and theme, manifesting varied degrees of power, but all exhibiting the peculiar directness and earnestness of the man.

The Harvest Time is his theme, and he calls flowers "the thoughts of God solidified," and the seasons "the four evangelists" of the earthly temple. He talks of Songs in the Night, and tells us "any fool can sing in the day. It is easy enough for an Ǽolian harp to whisper music when the winds blow; the difficulty is for music to come when no wind bloweth. It is easy to sing when we can read the notes by daylight; but the skillful singer is he who can sing when there is not a ray of light to read by—who sings from his heart, and not from a book that he can see."

But we have no space for the several passages we had marked for publication, and must refer the reader to the volume itself, assuring him that, while he will find somewhat to condemn, he will be rewarded with much of original and beautiful thought, set forth with an earnestness that leaves the magnetic power of their author no mystery. Marred, as these discourses are, with forms of expression that the disciples of Alison and Burke would deem sins against taste and beauty, and the believers in Whateley condemn, yet there is more than enough to disarm criticism. Some hand may be needed "to lop the wanton growth," but time, no doubt, will turn, for the once, his scythe into a pruning-hook. As to the precise character of this new light in the firmament of the religious world, we cannot speak; whether it will disappear as suddenly as it has flashed forth, is no question for our answering. One thing is certain: it did not rise as the stars do, but burst out all at once, and was well up before anybody had descried a dawn. The popular fear of comets everywhere is based, not so much upon their magnitude or the length of their trains, as upon the suddenness of their appearance, and the doubtful route of their orbits.

FROM THE REV. E.G. ROBINSON, D.D., PROFESSOR OF BIBLICAL AND PASTORAL THEOLOGY IN ROCHESTER UNIVERSITY

Messrs. Sheldon, Blakeman & Co.,

Gentlemen: Many thanks for your new volume of Spurgeon. I opened it with a good deal of misgiving, but must confess to a most agreeable surprise. It is an extremely rare thing that the sermons of a popular preacher will bear reading; but these of Spurgeon are not only better arranged and more logical than I had expected, but with soundness of doctrine; are also written in true Bunyan-like simplicity, directness and beauty. I am not surprised at his popularity, and am only glad it is so well founded. I shall recommend them to the attention of my class, and shall take up one or two of them for analysis, as a special exercise.

Respectfully yours,
E.G. Robinson

FROM FRANCIS WATLAND, D.D.

Providence, December 15, 1856

Gentlemen: When I wrote you last, I was reading Spurgeon's sermons. I have now finished them; and I thank God that such a preacher has been raised up to teach us how to address men on the subject of their salvation. I am surprised at their eloquence, but especially at the source of it. They are the result of a most thorough reading of the New Testament by a man of very remarkable gifts as a public speaker. They are the simple truths of the New Testament brought home to the consciences of men with a simplicity, honesty, fearlessness and affection, such as I have rarely, if ever witnessed.

P. Wayland

FROM THE REV. S. IRENÆUS PRIME, D.D.

New York, February 23, 1857

Messrs. Sheldon, Blakeman & Co.,

I am indebted to you for the pleasure of reading several of the sermons you propose to publish of the Rev. Mr. Spurgeon. They are far more able, interesting, and instructive; freer from coarseness and extravagance, and more evangelical and Scriptural than I had supposed from the notices I had read of his preaching. These sermons have the root of the matter in them, while their fervid style, earnest appeal, and vivid illustration, arrest the attention and impress the truth. The Rev. Dr. Campbell, of London, is the editor of the *British Banner*. He is the valiant opponent of the "Negative Theology" now infesting the dissenting churches of England. In his paper, he says of Mr. Spurgeon: "That young minister has more knowledge of the sacred Scriptures, the source of all genuine theology, than the whole of his traducers multiplied by the highest figure of the table. Nay, he is a better theologian than was either Grimshaw, or Berridge, or Whitefield, or Wesley, at the outset of their respective careers, and inferior to none of them at the close." I shall be pleased to commend the volume to the public when you bring it out.

Truly, yours,

S.L Prime